famous FAILS!

MIGHTY MISTAKES, MEGA MISHAPS & HOW A MESS CAN LEAD TO SUCCESS!

CRISPIN BOYER

NATIONAL GEOGRAPHIC

WASHINGTON, D.C.

Contents

CHAPTER SIX

Malfunctioning Mischief   **78**

CHAPTER SEVEN

Pop Culture Catastrophes   **92**

CHAPTER EIGHT

Lessons in Losing   **104**

Don't feel ashamed when you shout these words.

They're the rallying cries of nice tries: races lost, quizzes flunked, bikes wrecked, slipups and strikeouts, goofs and screwups—any misadventures that end in that forbidden word (so we'll just spell it out): F-A-L-U-R-E. Wait, did we get that wrong? Uh-oh!

Oh, relax. Some people might strike the word from their vocabulary, but failure is an overhated phenomenon. The ancient Greeks started a school of philosophy known as Stoicism, in which they braced for worst-case scenarios and faced their failures. Anyone who went through life expecting everything to go right, the Stoics figured, would have an extra-bad day when things went wrong. And failure still has its fans today—leaders, inventors, actors, and athletes who see it as a tool instead of that-thing-that-must-not-be-named. As superstar slugger

Babe Ruth once said, "Every strike brings me closer to the next home run."

This book celebrates the strikes: history's wrong turns, food flubs, malfunctioning monuments, inventions that fizzled, pop culture disasters, sorry sports moments, and so many more snafus that are funny because they're true. Along with some belly laughs, you'll get the scoops behind each oops: what went wrong, what went right, and what you can learn from it. In this book, failure *is* an option!

Getting the Most From *Famous Fails!*

Keep an eye peeled for these features as you read this book ...

Lesson Learned

Messing up can be a learning experience and a stomach-churning experience. Each tale of failure will offer advice for your own life. You'll walk away from *Famous Fails* a little smarter, with a boost of confidence, and less afraid of messing up!

It Could Be Worse!

If you're having a lousy day, just remember it's probably not as bad as what happened to some people in these stories.

Down but Not Out!

Believe it or not, some of the world's grade A success stories started out as grade F failures. Read about their horrible origin stories and incredible comebacks!

Triumphant Takeaway

From minor setbacks to complete disasters, there's always a hidden lesson that can help you avoid similar flubs in the future.

Are *you* a master messer-upper or a fantastic fixer?

See if you can spot the nine mistakes hidden in this book. (The answers are on page 120, but don't peek!)

"I have not failed
10,000 times;
I've **successfully found**
10,000 ways that
will not work."

—Thomas Edison, inventor of the lightbulb

CHAPTER ONE

Inadequate INVENTIONS

THE LIGHTBULB, the printing press, the automobile, the waffle iron—great inventions change the world, make impossible tasks a snap, or create an awesome breakfast. This chapter isn't about any of that stuff. Instead, get ready for a review of goofy gadgets and senseless contraptions—and meet the mad scientists behind them.

A Flying Compact Car?

NOT QUITE!

Look, up in the sky! It's a plane! It's a bird! It's a ... a Ford Pinto?

In the early 1970s, an American inventor named Henry Smolinski bolted the wings and engine of a small airplane to the body of a compact Ford automobile. Named the Mizar, his prototype had potential. Pilots could drive their Mizar-compatible car to the airport, install its wings, fly to a faraway airstrip, remove the wings, and cruise away. But Smolinski's flight of fancy had an altitude problem ...

HOT WHEELS
The Mizar prototype used a Ford Pinto fitted with flight controls cleverly designed to resemble a normal steering wheel and pedals. Pilots steered the plane with the wheel, pushing or pulling it to change altitude. The car's engine and brakes shortened takeoffs and landings.

HOT WINGS
The Mizar's wings had retractable legs that held it in place when parked. Drivers simply backed into the wing module, secured it to the car, connected the control cables, and taxied to the runway, ready for takeoff. The entire process was supposed to take two minutes. The plan was for the wing module to fit a variety of compatible cars.

FINAL FLIGHT

A 1973 test flight nearly ended in disaster when the strut holding the Mizar's right wing broke soon after takeoff. Fortunately, the test pilot managed to land the car, and he simply drove it back to the airport. Sadly, several months later, during the test flight of a new prototype, Smolinski was not as lucky when the strut problem struck again. This time the wing snapped off and the Mizar crashed. Smolinski was at the wheel, along with a friend in the passenger seat. Neither man survived. Though Smolinski's Mizar never really took off (no pun intended), he will be remembered as a brave inventor who risked it all in the name of science.

Lesson Learned

MAYBE THE MIZAR wasn't ready for takeoff, but you could still learn a lot from its wild ride and the man who made it. For starters, don't overload yourself!

Like the Mizar's wings, which weren't strong enough to carry a compact car, you have limits, too. Maybe you don't have the time to tackle a new after-school sport, or you might lack the extra bucks to start a new hobby. Pushing yourself past these limits once in a while is fine—and can even teach you new things about yourself—but don't overdo it. You might spread yourself too thin. Figure out what's most important and then prioritize. When the more important parts of your life begin to drag, don't hesitate to ease back on less important parts. Focus on less and you might achieve more.

 TRIUMPHANT TAKEAWAY We all have limits. It's important to know your own.

A Scooter That Will Change the World?

YEAH RIGHT!

It was a hovercraft! A new power source! An invention that would revolutionize transportation! Rumors swirled around the most mysterious machine of 2001, developed in secret by a famous inventor. It even had a code name: "It." Unveiled at the end of the year, "It" turned out to be the Segway: a stand-up scooter that was supposed to upgrade how we get around. Take a spin on one of the most overhyped inventions of all time ...

THE WHEEL THING

The Segway is an electric two-wheeled "personal transporter" that's a cinch to operate and nearly impossible to topple thanks to a high-tech system of computerized gyroscopes. To control direction, the driver simply leans forward or backward and turns the handlebars. The computer senses the driver's movements and handles the rest. Its inventor, Dean Kamen, predicted the Segway would "be to the car what the car was to the horse and buggy."

HYPE MACHINE

Inventor Kamen believed the Segway would be a hit with delivery companies and police departments, amusement parks and city commuters. But the scooter went nowhere. It was expensive (nearly $5,000), exceedingly heavy, and it suffered from a short battery life and limited range. It was also illegal to drive on many sidewalks around the world and was too slow for the street—factors that worked against its promise to replace the car for short trips. It didn't help that people looked silly leaning willy-nilly as they drove the thing. Though the contraptions have proved useful for tourists and law enforcement, Kamen initially hoped that his factory would be churning out 10,000 Segways a week. Instead, his company sold only 30,000 machines over the next six years.

Lesson Learned

MANAGE THE EXPECTATIONS of others. Segway inventor Kamen realized too late that his invention could never live up to the buzz. By developing it in secret, letting speculation run wild, and building expectations with bold comments, Kamen set the Segway hype machine spinning out of control.

Too much hype is rarely helpful in your own life. Bragging about your big brain or mad dancing skills or flawless three-point-shooting abilities will only amp up expectations. It's better to underpromise and overdeliver. Think about it: If your best is better than the expectations you set, you'll be a hit!

AUTO DESTRUCT Three Sorry Cars

Amphicar: Developed in 1961 to drive on roads and water, this fishy car sprung leaks and traveled as fast as a rowboat going upriver.

Edsel: Like the Segway, the Ford Edsel was a decent driving machine cursed by a high price and too much prelaunch hype.

Pinto: The Ford Pinto's run of rotten luck didn't end with the crash of the Mizar. The 1971 model could explode when struck from behind by another car.

 TRIUMPHANT TAKEAWAY Hype is overrated. Your good ideas sell themselves!

Virtual Reality in 1995?

Mario, Nintendo's mustached mascot, topples more turtles and rescues more pals by the end of level one than most video game heroes manage during an entire game. But not even this plump plumber could add extra life to the doomed Virtual Boy, a goggle-shaped three-dimensional gaming system launched in 1995 with many flaws ...

SEEING RED

Although the Virtual Boy could display 3-D graphics through its binocular visor, those graphics came in just two colors—red and black. Players complained of eyestrain and aching brains after staring at the dark, stark visuals.

VIRTUAL UNREALITY

Despite its name, the Virtual Boy failed to deliver an experience resembling virtual reality, which at the time existed only in movies and high-end arcades.

SALE FAIL

The Virtual Boy's initial price was $180—as much as a stand-alone console. Gamers could rent the system for $10 from certain stores, but few wanted to buy the Virtual Boy after trying it. It became Nintendo's only flop.

LAME GAMES

Consumers felt the Virtual Boy's library of games was lacking in quality—apparently, the included Mario Tennis was one of the few fun-to-play titles—and quantity (fewer than 15 games launched).

Lesson Learned

TIMING IS EVERYTHING! Sure, your idea might be awesome, but it still might flop if your timing isn't right.

Nintendo launched the Virtual Boy when virtual-reality technology was still too pricey and primitive for the living room. It was like building a television in the 1800s—an idea way ahead of its time.

Always take timing into account when considering your own big decisions. Is now the best time to buy a new gadget when the next big thing is just months away? Would you rather fight the crowds to see a cool new movie on opening night or wait for the hype to die down? Should you ask Mom to buy you a top-of-the-line TV if she just spent a fortune fixing the family car? And even if you think your stand-up routine is *hilarious*, it might be best to wait until after your big sister gets off the phone to perform it. Rushing into something can put you on the fast track to Failtown.

 TRIUMPHANT TAKEAWAY Being first isn't always best.

Four Failed Inventions

OH NO!

Lame inventions usually die on the drawing board, but somehow these four flawed ideas made it all the way to the real world. And one even caused injuries! Fear not: They're off the market today, but that doesn't mean we can't look back and have a laugh.

ANTI-BANDIT BAG

The pitch: Befuddle robbers with this briefcase that packs a surprise.

The reality: Pulling a chain in the bag's handle released a trapdoor that showered the sidewalk with everything inside. Meant to startle thieves, the anti-bandit bag only made it easier for them to grab your goodies.

BABY CAGES

The pitch: Let your little brother or sister enjoy a breath of fresh air—without having to leave the house!

The reality: Invented in the 1920s for busy parents living in small apartments in big cities, the baby cage was bolted to the walls outside high-rise windows and worked like a sort of open-air playpen. Daredevil toddlers could play with toys or spend nap time suspended dozens of stories above the ground. These cages were supposed to offer the health benefits of fresh air and sunshine—if the poor kids inside them didn't pass out from fear of heights.

WOW! CHIPS

The pitch: Chomp as many of these chips—fried in a special oil substitute named Olestra—as you want and never put on any pounds.

The reality: Olestra delivered the savory flavor of chips fried in oil, but this guiltless pleasure came with a gross side effect: "abdominal cramping and loose stools." In less medical-sounding terms: The chips might necessitate a trot to the toilet if you gobbled too many too quickly.

LAWN DARTS

The pitch: In this game designed as an alternative to horseshoes, players take turns tossing oversize darts with metal tips underhanded toward circular targets laid on the lawn.

The reality: Once tossed high into the air, the specially weighted darts returned to Earth spike first with enough force to cause serious injury. Nearly 5,000 kids wound up in emergency rooms after getting hit by falling darts. The dangerous game was banned in 1988.

 TRIUMPHANT TAKEAWAY Good intentions don't always lead to good results.

Smelly Movies?

HANS LAUBE

MIKE TODD, JR.

Before high-definition 3-D, titanic IMAX screens, and booming surround sound, theater tycoons tried all sorts of gimmicks to get audiences to buy tickets. The two most famous tricks made theaters smell and seats shake.

FRAGRANT FILM

We've all seen films that stunk, but what about a movie that makes you hold your nose? In 1960, director Mike Todd, Jr., introduced Smell-o-Vision: a machine that fanned odors to the noses of theater audiences. Smell-o-Vision held bottles of distinct scents, each released at specific times of the film. It wasn't the first theater-scent system, believe it or not, but Smell-o-Vision was the most advanced. Three theaters were equipped with the machine, and Todd produced a special movie called *Scent of Mystery* to showcase his technology. He insisted that Smell-o-Vision would be a "scentsation."

But technical glitches ruined its reception with critics and audiences. Scents triggered late or were too light to detect, and the machine's hissing delivery distracted audiences from a movie that was about as captivating as watching bread bake (*Scent of Mystery* actually contains a scene of bread baking). No other Smell-o-Vision films were produced, although the idea pops up from time to time today in everything from movie theaters to smartphone apps.

Lesson Learned

ADD SUBSTANCE TO YOUR STYLE. Both Smell-o-Vision and Percepto (see opposite) flopped because they were forgettable gimmicks—flashy tricks with no real content to back them up (although watching bread bake might be entertaining if you're hungry).

Whenever you begin a project, such as writing a short story, shooting a video, or assembling a science project, you want to both wow your audience and keep them wanting more. While a cool gimmick can get people talking about your project, you'll lose them if you don't follow up with a good story or relatable characters or something that adds depth and excitement to the experience.

18

Electrified Seats?

SHOCKING CINEMA

Director William Castle, a filmmaker famous for outlandish gimmicks (he once planted screaming actors in the audience for his horror movies), was a maestro at building audience buzz. For his 1959 horror film *The Tingler*, he literally buzzed his audience.

The Tingler features a parasite that lives in the human spine and delivers tingling sensations when its host feels fright. Wanting his audience to experience what they saw on the screen, Castle developed "Percepto," a system of electrical buzzers placed under theater seats. At the climax of the film, in a scene when the Tingler escapes into a theater, the Percepto system began jolting the backsides of audience members. But the Percepto buzzers were about as shocking as a cell phone vibrating in your back pocket. Audiences shrugged their shoulders and kept munching their popcorn.

WHEN THE SCREEN SCREAMS YOU'LL SCREAM TOO... IF YOU VALUE YOUR LIFE!

PERCEPTO! newest and most startling gimmick on the screen!...

COLUMBIA PICTURES presents

The Tingler

GUARANTEED
"The Tingler" will break loose in the theatre while you are in the audience. As you enter the theatre you will receive instructions... how to guard yourself against attack by THE TINGLER!

starring VINCENT PRICE
with JUDITH EVELYN
DARRYL HICKMAN · PATRICIA CUTTS
Written by ROBB WHITE · Produced and Directed by WILLIAM CASTLE
A WILLIAM CASTLE PRODUCTION

 TRIUMPHANT TAKEAWAY Gimmicks are good. Gimmicks mixed with good ideas are better.

Happy Accidents

OOPS!

Toy successes that started as something less ...

PLAY-DOH

Original intention: Wallpaper cleaner
Roll it into snakes, sculpt it into shapes, assemble the pieces into beasts, then mash it all up and start over. The colorful clay Play-Doh is a beloved toy today, but it was created in 1933 by Ohio inventor Noah McVicker for a dirty job: to clean coal soot from wallpaper (coal was once a common heating fuel for houses, and its dust stuck to everything).

When coal fell out of use in the 1950s, demand for wallpaper cleaner plunged with it, and McVicker's soap company, Kutol Products, was bound for bankruptcy. That is until his nephew Joe heard that children were molding the wall cleaner into shapes. He had an idea! He tweaked the nontoxic recipe, added its unique scent, and—voilà!— Play-Doh was born. Today, about 95 million cans sell each year in 75 countries around the world. That's a lot of snakes!

THE SLINKY

Original intention: Shock absorber

"What walks down stairs, alone or in pairs, and makes a slinkity sound?" Even if you don't know its catchy jingle, you've probably played with a Slinky. This stair-stepping metal spring became an international sensation that evolved into plastic models and the Slinky Dog made famous in the film *Toy Story*. But before it hit toy stores, the Slinky had a previous life as a normal spring in the workshop of a shipbuilding company in Philadelphia, Pennsylvania, U.S.A.

Engineer Richard James was working on ways to stabilize sensitive battleship equipment when he accidentally knocked the spring off a shelf. Inspiration struck as he watched it slink to the ground: It might make a great toy! James's wife, Betty, paged through a dictionary for the perfect name.

She settled on "Slinky" due to the toy's slinking movements and swishing sound. The first 400 Slinkys sold out in 90 minutes just before Christmas in 1945. Enough Slinkys have sold since to wrap around Earth 150 times.

Lesson Learned

WHEN YOU HIT A DEAD END, try heading in a new direction. Neither the Slinky nor Play-Doh would exist today if their inventors hadn't transformed them from tools into toys. They had imagination. They had vision. They had friends and family help them see their inventions from fresh perspectives.

The good news is, you have all those tools, too! Apply some imagination and vision to your failures—and invite some second opinions from friends—and you might turn a bad idea into a brilliant one (or at least learn how to avoid making the same mistake again).

 TRIUMPHANT TAKEAWAY Sometimes mistakes can lead to something great!

Down but Not Out!

[THOMAS EDISON]

Before achieving success, this genius inventor tried, tried, tried again ... and again and again!

A brilliant tinkerer, Thomas Edison figured out how to harness electricity to light a filament in a glass bulb. That may not sound so special until you discover that his brightest idea became the first commercially successful lightbulb. Most inventors would hang up their tinkering tools and call it a career after achieving such a feat, but Edison went on to develop a type of movie projector and the phonograph (sort of the great-granddaddy of your portable media player).

With more than a thousand patents to his name, he helped usher in an age of innovation in the 19th century. But before he helped light up the world, Edison went through some dark times.

TOP FLOPS Edison's Epic Fails

Edison's early years were filled with failed inventions and missteps in creating the lightbulb. Lowlights include ...

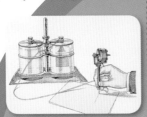

The Electric Pen
Instead of writing in ink, this battery-operated pen poked holes in wax paper, creating a stencil for multiple copies. The heavy gadget made a racket—and a big mess.

The Talking Doll
Edison developed a tiny version of his phonograph and stuffed it into a doll, but the device was much too fragile for children's playtime. Its scratchy voice also made it sound like a doll from a horror movie.

The Kinetophone
A sort of personal movie theater, the Kinetophone displayed films through a peephole. You think watching movies on your smartphone is hard—imagine hunching over the Kinetophone for two hours.

Lesson Learned

DON'T DWELL ON YOUR MISTAKES.
Just imagine if Thomas Edison had stopped to worry about all of his failures. He never would have had time to dream up his successes!

Beating yourself up over every setback not only makes you feel lousy, it's also counterproductive. Inspiration won't strike if you're too busy moping around. Think about what you did wrong, learn from the experience, and then move on to your next bright idea.

TRIUMPHANT TAKEAWAY You're only a failure if you quit trying!

"Only the one who **does not question** is safe from making a mistake."

—Albert Einstein

CHAPTER TWO

Sordid PAST

IT'S A BUMMER when you botch something in your own life, but at least the embarrassment isn't etched in stone. Just shrug off the stung feelings and treat yourself to a banana split. A barge of banana splits couldn't erase this chapter's epic failures, however. Mistaken destinations, conquered capitals, scientific slipups—these enduring disasters are ones for the history books!

Forgot to Guard the Gate?

UH-OH!

You've probably done it at least once: accidentally left a gate unlatched or the back door unlocked. Maybe the dog got out. Maybe Mom or Dad lectured you on responsibility. It was a boneheaded move, sure, but it wasn't the end of the world. But in 1453, for the residents of the besieged city Constantinople, an unlocked gate really did lead to the end of their world ...

ENEMY AT THE GATE

Straddling Europe and Asia, capital city of the Eastern Roman Empire (or Byzantine Empire), Constantinople was prime real estate during the Middle Ages, from the 5th to the 15th centuries A.D. Everyone wanted a piece of this cultural crossroads, home to amazing palaces, towering domes, and a convenient harbor. Surrounded by a double ring of stone walls, Constantinople shrugged off more than 20 sieges from some of history's most fearsome forces: barbarians and Attila the Hun. The Byzantine Empire began to wane in influence in the 15th century, but its capital city seemed invincible.

Sultan Mehmed II of the rival Ottoman Empire believed otherwise. In 1453, he led a vast army and navy against the city, blasting its walls with the largest cannons yet wielded in battle. Despite his superior numbers and firepower, however, Mehmed II seemed unlikely to conquer this city that had survived so many previous sieges.

That's when Ottoman soldiers made an astounding discovery. The city's residents had forgotten to lock a small gate called the Kerkoporta, used by the defenders to launch counterattacks from the walls. The Ottoman soldiers, no doubt gobsmacked at finding it open and undefended, flooded through the gate and quickly raised their flag. The city fell into panic. Constantinople came under the control the Ottomans, marking the fall of one empire and the rise of a new one. The city flourished under Ottoman rule for more than 450 years. Some historians even suspect that people in Constantinople intentionally left the Kerkoporta unlocked because they were ready for a change. The city was renamed Istanbul in 1923 with the founding of the Republic of Turkey.

ATTILA THE HUN

SULTAN MEHMED II

Lesson Learned

DETAILS MATTER. The fall of Constantinople sent shock waves through history, altering the courses of countries, religions, and wars. The world might be very different today if Constantinople's defenders had just remembered to lock the Kerkoporta.

Likewise, neglecting the small details in your own life could lead to some unintended consequences. Skip oiling the chain on your bicycle and you might end up walking home somewhere down the road. Forget to invite a friend to a party today and you could end up with hurt feelings on your hands. Leave your game system plugged in during a thunderstorm and it might get zapped. You don't need to sweat every minor detail, of course, but paying attention to the little things could pay off—or at least spare you a lecture from your parents about forgetting to lock the gate.

TRIUMPHANT TAKEAWAY A little extra care could save you from making big mistakes.

Newton Messed Up His Math?

OH NO!

Sir Isaac Newton was one of history's most influential minds: a scientist who literally wrote the books on physics, a mathematician who helped invent the study of calculus, and a philosopher famous for sitting in a garden and spotting an apple falling from a tree (an observation that inspired his law of universal gravitation). But this English genius made a goof that went unnoticed for more than 300 years—until it was spotted by a student.

PHILOSOPHIÆ
NATURALIS
PRINCIPIA
MATHEMATICA.

Autore JS. NEWTON, Trin. Coll. Cantab. Soc. Matheseos
Professore Lucasiano, & Societatis Regalis Sodali.

IMPRIMATUR·
S. PEPYS, Reg. Soc. PRÆSES.
Julii 5. 1686.

LONDINI,

Jussu Societatis Regiæ ac Typis Josephi Streater. Prostat apud
plures Bibliopolas. Anno MDCLXXXVII.

NUMBER CRUNCHER

When Robert Garisto, a 23-year-old senior at the University of Chicago, focused on one of Newton's equations while writing a class paper, something didn't add up. The equation—straight from one of Newton's most famous books on physics—was meant to demonstrate important details about the planets, including their gravity at the surface and mass (similar to weight). But Newton's equation had a typo. It used data that didn't match Newton's own explanation of the equation. Garisto was a little shocked at the mistake, but he believed that finding it was just part of the assignment. He pointed it out in his paper and turned it in.

Turns out Garisto had just discovered a discrepancy that no one had noticed for three centuries. His feat earned him a prestigious prize from a scientific honor society. And, of course, he got an A plus on the paper.

ROBERT GARISTO

Lesson Learned

YOU HAVE A UNIQUE PERSPECTIVE; use it to make unique observations. University student Robert Garisto caught the discrepancy in Newton's equation because he looked at it in a new way—as a problem that needed solving. Sometimes you'll make what you think are obvious observations (such as friends acting strangely or problems with a plan) that only you see because of your unique perspective. You might have expertise or knowledge that people around you lack, or maybe you're just an especially observant person. Regardless, don't always assume that everyone else sees what you do. Ask people you can trust if they notice the same things and maybe you'll help someone with their situation—or even solve a centuries-old mystery.

TRIUMPHANT TAKEAWAY What seems obvious to you might not be to everyone else.

Found a Phony Island

a

History's greatest explorers are as famous for their mixed-up destinations as for their adventures. Christopher Columbus mistook the island of Cuba for the coast of China. English explorer Henry Hudson spent years exploring the eastern coast of North America for a trade route to Asia that didn't exist. Spanish conquistador Ponce de León, according to legend, discovered Florida while searching for the Fountain of Youth. You could hardly blame them for getting lost. Instead of GPS or Google Maps, they had to create their own maps! And their mistakes stuck. The result: phantom islands, or lands that appeared on old maps but turned out to be mirages, incorrectly drawn, or outright mythical. Hop aboard for a high-seas tour of some of the most famous examples ...

THE ISLAND OF CALIFORNIA

It's hard to believe that California, the third largest U.S. state, could be mistaken for an island—but that's how it appeared on maps for more than 200 years! History's most famous map mistake started when a Spanish sailor named Fortún Ximénez landed on the southern tip of Baja in 1533. He mistook the peninsula for an island and decided to name it the Island of California, after a fictional paradise from a Spanish novel. The fiction was taken for fact, and California was drawn as an island on many maps until the 18th century.

SANDY ISLAND

Until 2012, you could've spotted this tiny speck of an island off the eastern coast of Australia in Google Maps and in atlases—but you could never have visited it. Charted in 1774 by British explorer Captain James Cook, Sandy Island made headlines in 2012 when it was "undiscovered" by an Australian survey ship. It likely never existed (Cook may have mistaken a mass of drifting pumice as an island).

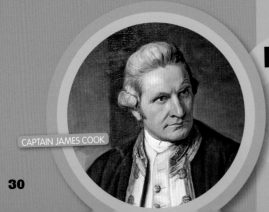

CAPTAIN JAMES COOK

HY-BRASIL

A phantom island in every sense of the word, Hy-Brasil was a fabled land allegedly hidden in mist that only cleared for one day every seven years. It appeared on maps off the western coast of Ireland as far back as the 14th century. Expeditions to find Hy-Brasil were unsuccessful, unless you count the astounding story of Captain John Nisbet. He claimed to have found the island populated with massive black rabbits and a magician living in a castle, conjuring mist to hide the island.

ISLAND OF DEMONS

The name conjures images of wild beasts devouring marooned sailors. Fear not! The "Island of Demons"—which first appeared on maps off the coast of Newfoundland, Canada, in the 16th century—doesn't actually exist. It grew from the legend of a captain's niece who claimed she was marooned on the island and tormented by demons.

Lesson Learned

TRY TO SEE THE BIG PICTURE. Strange as it may sound, you have something in common with early explorers. Just as they charted an uncertain course around phantom islands, misshapen continents, and hidden reefs, you navigate through life using an incomplete map. Friends might mysteriously turn unfriendly. People might whisper when you enter a room. Your parents might start acting strangely.

Instead of jumping to conclusions or believing every rumor you hear, try to fill in the blanks of what you know and put together a more accurate picture of what's really going on. Talk to the friends you're having problems with. Listen to what they have to say. Observe the people around you. By talking, listening, and observing, you're acting like an explorer in your own life, filling in the map and charting a course you can count on.

 TRIUMPHANT TAKEAWAY You don't know everything, and that's okay!

Picked the Wrong President?

UH-OH!

You can't believe everything you read, and this story is proof of that. According to a major newspaper, the 33rd president of the United States was one defeated Democrat.

 It's a famous photo snapped in 1948: U.S. president Harry Truman is all smiles as he holds up a *Chicago Daily Tribune* newspaper with a headline declaring his defeat in the recent presidential election. Why would this loser look so happy? Simple: He actually won. In its rush to be first with the news, the newspaper got its facts wrong. Here's the true story of the history's most famous false headline ...

OOPS SCOOP

In the days before online journalism and the instant fixes of website updates, mistakes lived forever in black-and-white newsprint. Deadlines could spell disaster. Case in point: "Dewey Defeats Truman." The banner headline stretched across the front page of the *Chicago Daily Tribune* on November 3, 1948, the day after Harry Truman actually defeated candidate Thomas Dewey.

A swarm of mishaps led to the front page's mistaken identity, every publisher's worst-case scenario. Because of a printers' strike, the paper went to press earlier than usual and before all the election tallies were in. *Daily Tribune* editors relied on the expertise of its own Washington, D.C., correspondent and the results of voter polls, which predicted a clear victory for Dewey.

The polls were wrong, and the heated race ended with the reelection of incumbent Truman. That was after 150,000 copies of the *Tribune* had run with the embarrassing headline, immortalized two days later when a victorious Truman held up a copy for that famous photo.

Chicago Daily Tribune

DEWEY DEFEATS TRUMAN

G.O.P. Sweep Indicated in State; Boyle Leads in City

KENTUCKY

DEWEY WILL WIN

REPUBLICAN CONVENTION, 1948

Lesson Learned

IF A FLUB IS FIXABLE, FIX IT FAST! Once it became clear that Truman had won the election, the next edition of the *Tribune* ran a story with the correct info. The editors acted quickly, and the publishers showed they had a sense of humor by embracing their big mistake as part of the newspaper's history. They even created a plaque replicating the headline as a gift for Truman 25 years later. Follow the *Tribune*'s example. If you accidentally hurt someone's feelings, apologize pronto. If you broke a window, use your allowance to pay for repairs. Letting flubs linger only spreads out the damage. Remember, each failure you fix takes you one step closer to success.

 TRIUMPHANT TAKEAWAY Mistakes lose their sting if you correct them quickly.

Wrecked Your Rocket?

OOPS!

Liftoff! Riding atop a pillar of fire, the Mariner 1 space probe rocketed from its Florida, U.S.A., launch pad in July 1962. Next stop: Venus! But NASA's first planet-probing spacecraft went haywire almost immediately. The booster's guidance system started steering the craft back toward Earth, forcing NASA controllers to hit the destruct button. Kaboom! The $80 million probe blew to bits less than five minutes after liftoff—and all because of a typing mistake.

MISSION TO VENUS

Humanity's first steps into space started as a race between the United States and the former Soviet Union, rivals in a global struggle for power. And the Soviets—who had sent the first human into orbit in 1961—were winning. Engineers at NASA, the U.S. space agency, were determined to win the next leg of the space race with unmanned voyages to planets in the solar system. So began the Mariner program of planetary probes. But in the rush to be first, someone at NASA messed up.

HYPHEN HATED

According to NASA's own investigation of the Mariner 1 failure, the probe's booster went rogue because of a typo in the launch program. Someone accidentally left out a hyphen (or a similar symbol called a crossbar) while inputting the complex computer code that was guiding the launch. That single omission sent the rocket off course. As sci-fi author Arthur C. Clarke later wrote, Mariner 1 was "wrecked by the most expensive hyphen in history."

It Could Be Worse!

WHEN YOU'RE HAVING A LOUSY DAY, just be glad you weren't a member of NASA's navigation team for the Mars Climate Orbiter. The unmanned probe was launched to study the red planet's atmosphere in 1999. But it got a little too close, burning up in the Martian atmosphere because the guidance team used the metric system for its calculations instead of the standard measurements used by the probe's builders. That simple math problem spelled doom for the $328 million craft.

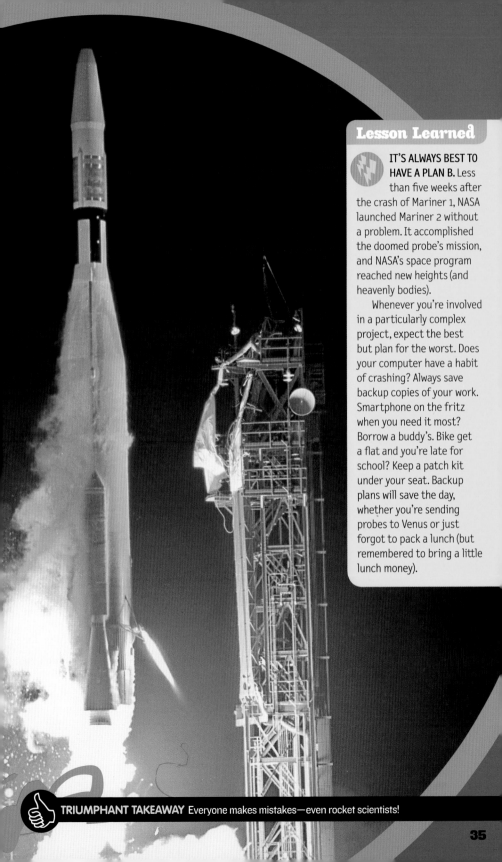

Lesson Learned

IT'S ALWAYS BEST TO HAVE A PLAN B. Less than five weeks after the crash of Mariner 1, NASA launched Mariner 2 without a problem. It accomplished the doomed probe's mission, and NASA's space program reached new heights (and heavenly bodies).

Whenever you're involved in a particularly complex project, expect the best but plan for the worst. Does your computer have a habit of crashing? Always save backup copies of your work. Smartphone on the fritz when you need it most? Borrow a buddy's. Bike get a flat and you're late for school? Keep a patch kit under your seat. Backup plans will save the day, whether you're sending probes to Venus or just forgot to pack a lunch (but remembered to bring a little lunch money).

TRIUMPHANT TAKEAWAY Everyone makes mistakes—even rocket scientists!

Down but Not Out!

[ALBERT EINSTEIN]

There's a good reason we call smart people today "Einsteins." In the early 1900s, wild-haired physicist Albert Einstein laid the foundation for modern physics and our understanding of the relationship between time and space. But before he became famous for his brains, he suffered some major growing pains ...

PROBLEM CHILD

One of the most brilliant minds of the 20th century didn't have much to say during his earliest days. Einstein didn't begin speaking until he was four! His parents feared he had a learning disability. If he'd taken this long to start speaking, how would he handle school?

It's a popular myth that young Einstein was a bad student—that he even failed math classes. The truth is more complex. He was a rebellious but intensely curious boy who angered teachers with smart-aleck comments. Einstein was brilliant at math and understood complicated physics before his 11th birthday, but lousy grades in French and other non-math subjects held him back—which is why he ended up working in a Swiss patent office when he began formulating the theories that eventually won him the Nobel Prize in physics.

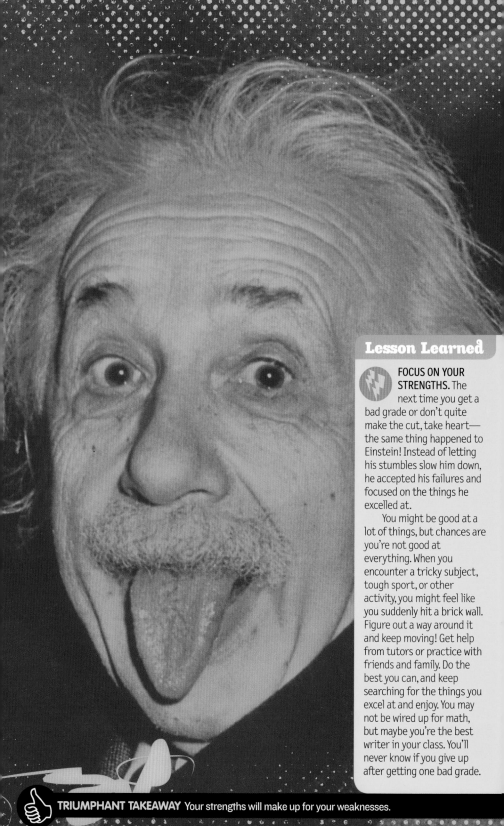

Lesson Learned

FOCUS ON YOUR STRENGTHS. The next time you get a bad grade or don't quite make the cut, take heart— the same thing happened to Einstein! Instead of letting his stumbles slow him down, he accepted his failures and focused on the things he excelled at.

You might be good at a lot of things, but chances are you're not good at everything. When you encounter a tricky subject, tough sport, or other activity, you might feel like you suddenly hit a brick wall. Figure out a way around it and keep moving! Get help from tutors or practice with friends and family. Do the best you can, and keep searching for the things you excel at and enjoy. You may not be wired up for math, but maybe you're the best writer in your class. You'll never know if you give up after getting one bad grade.

TRIUMPHANT TAKEAWAY Your strengths will make up for your weaknesses.

"The physician can bury his mistakes—but an architect can only advise his client to **plant vines** [to hide them]."

—Architect Frank Lloyd Wright

CHAPTER THREE

Botched BUILDINGS

WHEN IT COMES TO BUILDING BIG, there are no small mistakes. Bridges collapse. Monuments malfunction. Ships sink on their maiden voyages. In this chapter, you'll tour buildings with accidental heat rays and architectural wonders that turned into blunders. Better wear a hard hat. Some of these failures are as big as a house—or bigger.

A Skyscraper That Fries Eggs?

EPIC FAIL!

Scorched cars! Blistered bicycles! Singed streets! In 2013, London's financial district became a scene from a Godzilla movie with a silly twist. But in this story, the monster is actually a building.

BURNING BUILDING

Nicknamed the "Walkie-Talkie" because of its strange shape—skinny at the bottom, bulging up top—the 37-story office building at London's 20 Fenchurch Street created a hot mess halfway through its construction. The wall of shiny windows on its south side curve in a way that focuses the rays of the midday sun onto the street below.

HOT SPOT

For two hours each day during the summer, the Walkie-Talkie transforms into a magnifying glass, melting cars and scorching welcome mats in neighboring shops. Temperatures in the sunniest spot can reach the boiling point. To demonstrate Walkie-Talkie's hot spot, a journalist fried an egg on the sidewalk. Londoners came up with a new nickname for the skyscraper: Walkie-Scorchie.

REHEAT PERFORMANCE

This building's burning ability wasn't by design (architect Rafael Viñoly blamed last-minute design changes for the heat-ray effect). The Walkie-Talkie isn't even the first "fryscraper." Las Vegas's Vdara Hotel has a similar curved shape that melted plastic pool chairs and singed the hair of visitors until workers applied a special film to the windows. You already know its architect: Rafael Viñoly, the man behind the Walkie-Scorchie.

Lesson Learned

FIND A FUNCTION FOR YOUR MALFUNCTIONS. Walkie-Talkie architect Rafael Viñoly, for instance, has turned his street-heating design flaw into an ingenious solution: He designed a building in China that harnesses his sun-magnifying design to capture and use solar energy.

Whenever you mess up in your own life, try to dream up ways to salvage the situation. Maybe you can squeeze a laugh from an embarrassing situation or turn a wrong turn into an adventure.

TRIUMPHANT TAKEAWAY Embrace your mistakes. Failure can create new opportunities!

A Tower of Trouble?

UH-OH!

The lawn just south of Italy's Leaning Tower of Pisa had become a risky picnic spot by the 1990s. Computer models predicted that the tower was ready to tumble! Why is it still standing today? Let's set the record straight on this leaning landmark ...

TOURIST TRAP

With the top level overhanging the ground by 15 feet (4.6 m) and the tower on the brink of collapse, Italian officials closed the Leaning Tower of Pisa to tourists in 1990 for safety reasons. The government ordered a $30 million restoration project, turning the tower into a titanic fixer-upper.

REOPENING DAY!

With its lean declared stable, the Tower of Pisa reopened to tourists in December 2001. The lawn south of the tower was once again safe for picnickers and silly photo ops of tourists pretending to prop up the teetering tower.

FIXING IT WRONG

1250: Architects try to compensate for the tower's lean by adjusting its angle halfway through construction. They end up giving the tower a slight banana shape.

1934: Under orders of Italian leader Benito Mussolini, workers drill holes into the tower's base and load them with tons of cement. The fix does more damage than good, weakening the foundation and adding another tenth of a degree to the tilt.

1995: Workers freeze the ground beneath the tower to install anchoring cables, but the process creates underground gaps that cause a lurch in the tower's lean. Officials fear a collapse is imminent!

It Could Be Worse!

WHEN YOU'RE HAVING A LOUSY DAY,

just be glad you weren't Alessandro Della Gherardesca. In 1838, this architect dug up the base of the Tower of Pisa to show tourists its foundation. His excavation weakened the already soft soil, increasing the tower's tilt to the point of toppling.

FIXING IT RIGHT

1992: Engineers use steel cables to anchor the tower to a nearby building to prevent it from tipping during restoration efforts.

1993: Workers add hundreds of tons of lead weights to the north side of the tower to help tilt the landmark back in the correct direction.

1999: Corkscrewing into the soil with heavy drills, construction crews remove massive amounts of dirt from beneath the north side of the tower. Slowly, the tower begins to right itself to a safer angle.

Lesson Leraned

DON'T REJECT YOUR IMPERFECTIONS! The Tower of Pisa is a tourist hot-spot precisely because of its off-kilter charm. A chief requirement of Italy's $30 million tower-fixing effort in the 1990s, in fact, was that the tilt be kept intact. Your own quirks are no less valuable. Have an odd laugh? Mismatched eyes? A funny nose? These "flaws" make you you.

The Tower of Pisa's extreme lean inspired copies, such as the Leaning Tower of Niles, Illinois, U.S.A., a half-size version complete with its own tilt.

 TRIUMPHANT TAKEAWAY Perfection is overrated. Take pride in your quirks.

43

Blunders of the Ancient World

OH NO!

From the Great Wall of China to Egypt's Great Pyramid of Giza, ancient architects knew how to build big and leave their mark on history. But sometimes that mark ended up as more of a blemish. See for yourself in this tour of four ancient wonders that turned into blunders ...

FIDENAE STADIUM
ROME, ITALY

Roman citizens—as many as 50,000—crammed into the seats of this stadium to gawk at gladiator battles, beast hunts, and other gory spectacles. Unfortunately, the foundation and wooden structure weren't strong enough for so many spectators. As many as 20,000 people died when the stadium collapsed in 27 A.D., the deadliest sports disaster in history.

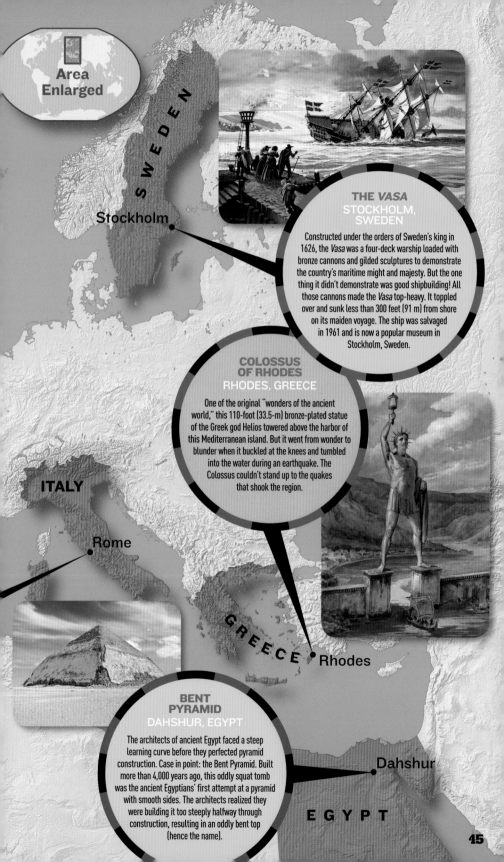

SWEDEN

Stockholm

ITALY

Rome

GREECE

Rhodes

THE *VASA*
STOCKHOLM,
SWEDEN

Constructed under the orders of Sweden's king in 1626, the *Vasa* was a four-deck warship loaded with bronze cannons and gilded sculptures to demonstrate the country's maritime might and majesty. But the one thing it didn't demonstrate was good shipbuilding! All those cannons made the *Vasa* top-heavy. It toppled over and sunk less than 300 feet (91 m) from shore on its maiden voyage. The ship was salvaged in 1961 and is now a popular museum in Stockholm, Sweden.

COLOSSUS OF RHODES
RHODES, GREECE

One of the original "wonders of the ancient world," this 110-foot (33.5-m) bronze-plated statue of the Greek god Helios towered above the harbor of this Mediterranean island. But it went from wonder to blunder when it buckled at the knees and tumbled into the water during an earthquake. The Colossus couldn't stand up to the quakes that shook the region.

BENT PYRAMID
DAHSHUR, EGYPT

The architects of ancient Egypt faced a steep learning curve before they perfected pyramid construction. Case in point: the Bent Pyramid. Built more than 4,000 years ago, this oddly squat tomb was the ancient Egyptians' first attempt at a pyramid with smooth sides. The architects realized they were building it too steeply halfway through construction, resulting in an oddly bent top (hence the name).

Dahshur

EGYPT

World's Tallest Empty Building?

EPIC FAIL!

You can't order room service at the Ryugyong Hotel. In fact, you can't even get a room. The hotel doesn't have any! This 105-story skyscraper in Pyongyang, the capital city of North Korea, holds the Guinness Record for the "world's tallest unoccupied building"—even though construction was completed in 1992. Here's the tall tale behind "the phantom hotel."

CROOKED CONSTRUCTION

Analysis of the hotel after its completion revealed serious problems, including a shoddy concrete shell and elevator shafts that didn't line up. The Ryugyong Hotel became the laughing stock of the architectural world, earning harsh nicknames such as the "hotel of doom" and "the worst building in the history of mankind."

TOWER OF TROUBLE

When construction began in 1987, the Ryugyong Hotel was planned to offer the ultimate in luxury accommodations: thousands of rooms, deluxe casinos, flashy nightclubs, and fancy restaurants on tippy-top floors that rotated to provide 360-degree views of the city. The hotel was supposed to open in 1989—which would have made it the world's tallest hotel at the time. Then the money ran out. As North Korea spiraled into an economic crisis with the breakup of its ally the Soviet Union, construction stopped in 1992. The building had reached its full height of 1,083 feet (330 m), but it was just a concrete skeleton with no doors, elevators, lights, bathrooms—or even windows.

TOWERING EMBARRASSMENT

Forever unfinished and an eyesore on the Pyongyang skyline (the stark construction has been compared to the Death Star in *Star Wars*), the Ryugyong Hotel became an eyesore and an embarrassment for North Korea's secretive leaders. They even digitally erased the tower from official photos of the city!

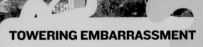

MONEY FOR NOTHING

Cost estimates for the construction of the Ryugyong Hotel run between 2 and 10 percent of the value of *everything* produced in North Korea.

EMPTY INSIDE

Construction resumed in 2008. By 2011, glass panels covered the concrete frame, and the hotel was supposed to open in 2013. But photos of the interior revealed the Ryugyong's dirty secret: It was just a concrete shell without furniture, doors, or light fixtures. At this hotel, nobody's home.

Lesson Learned

DON'T START what you can't finish. The Ryugyong Hotel was meant to display North Korea's wealth and power; instead, it serves as a monument to poor leadership and misdirected resources. Likewise, an unfinished project reflects badly on you. It shows that you can't manage your time, make a realistic plan, and stick to your word.

Before you announce to your friends and family that you plan to accomplish a particular goal (such as learning an instrument or building a tree house), determine whether you have the time and resources to achieve that goal. After all, wouldn't it be more satisfying to declare your mission is accomplished than to have to explain why you missed the mark?

 TRIUMPHANT TAKEAWAY Think big—as long as you think realistically.

A Bucking Bridge?

OOPS!

When workers installed the final rivets on the Tacoma Narrows Bridge in 1940, they had created an engineering marvel: the third largest suspension bridge in the world, spanning a deep stretch of Puget Sound, in Washington State, U.S.A., which was under assault from powerful currents and raging winds. Without knowing it, they had also built the world's most dangerous roller coaster—and its last drop was a doozy. Hang on tight for the rise and fall of "Galloping Gertie."

It Could Be Worse!

WHEN YOU'RE HAVING A LOUSY DAY,

just be glad you weren't Clark Eldridge, the engineer in charge of building the Tacoma Narrows Bridge. He rushed to the bridge the day of its collapse and watched it tumble into Puget Sound. "I go over the (new) Tacoma Bridge frequently and always with an ache in my heart," he later wrote in his memoir. "It was my bridge."

TWIST IN THE WIND

Not long after construction began on the bridge in 1938, workers noticed it had a stomach-churning habit of wobbling in strong winds. Some workers even complained of seasickness! They nicknamed the bridge "Galloping Gertie" for its bucking ability, and worked on ways to minimize the motion—none of which were successful.

GUST BUSTED

Just four months after the bridge was opened in 1940, strong gusts of around 40 miles an hour (64 km/h) began twisting the bridge, wringing it like a washcloth in the hands of an invisible giant. A college student named Winfield Brown thought it would be fun to cross the bucking bridge on foot—until he was thrown to the ground by its wild wobbling. Crawling on his hands and knees, he inched to safety and later described the ordeal as worse than any roller coaster.

Traffic stopped as the twisting grew worse. Cables snapped and concrete cracked. The last man off the bridge was a newspaper editor named Leonard Coatsworth. Thrown to the roadway after abandoning his car, he crawled off the span just in time to see it snap and plummet into Puget Sound.

Lesson Learned

LEARN FROM YOUR MISTAKES—or even the mistakes of others. Investigators of the Tacoma Narrows Bridge incident blamed its collapse partially on solid rails that caught the wind like a sail—something that engineers never thought would be a problem when they built the span. The crash became a course on how not to build a bridge, and all future suspension bridges were constructed with handrails that permitted the wind to pass through.

It just goes to show that you won't see some problems in life until they throw you for a loop. Friends move away. Pets get sick. These ordeals can come out of nowhere. Sometimes the best you can do is hang on and not give up.

 TRIUMPHANT TAKEAWAY Failure is the best teacher.

"Life will be up;
life will be down ...
You can laugh at it
or you can cry at it,
and laughing feels
better than crying."

—Celebrity chef Rachael Ray

CHAPTER FOUR

Bad TASTES

SUCCESS IS SWEET—everyone knows that—but what about the flavor of failure? Is it sweet? Sour? Tinged with fried pickle? Yes, yes, and—wait, what? FRIED PICKLE? Get ready to ruin your appetite: This chapter is a menu of food flops, taste bud bombardments, and recipes for disaster.

A New Formula for an Old Soda?

UH-OH!

Imagine if your favorite treat— chocolate chip cookies, for instance, or those jalapeño chips you can't stop munching—suddenly disappeared from store shelves and was replaced with ... something different. Cola aficionados faced such a crisis in April 1985, when the Coca-Cola Company announced it was changing the formula of its flagship soda pop. It is considered one of the greatest blunders in product history ...

 It Could Be Worse!

WHEN YOU'RE HAVING A LOUSY DAY,

just be glad you weren't Roberto Goizueta, who was Coca-Cola's chairman when New Coke was introduced. As the new formula hit shelves, he received letters calling him "Chief Dodo" and other snarky and horrible things.

TASTE OF SUCCESS

Invented by a pharmacist in 1886, Coca-Cola was originally sold at soda fountains for a nickel per glass as a healthy cure-all for headaches, anxiety, exhaustion—whatever ailed you. It was soon rebranded as a refreshing beverage, and clever advertising helped put the pop on top.

BOTTLE BATTLE

After World War II, Coke's competitors were ready to savor the flavor of victory. Pepsi grew in popularity thanks to "Pepsi Challenges" that showed that pop fans preferred Pepsi to Coke. By the 1980s, the "Cola Wars" were raging.

ENTER NEW COKE!

Coca-Cola tried to up its game. On April 23, 1985, the company debuted its new, sweeter formula, aka "New Coke," while halting production of the old formula. New Coke was preferred in taste tests of nearly 200,000 soda fans. Coke braced for a boost in sales and certain victory in the Cola Wars.

MORE LIKE "EWW, COKE!"

Judging by the public's reaction, you'd think Coke had just canceled their favorite soda. The company's phone lines were flooded with calls from outraged soda fans demanding the return of the original formula. Groups such as the "Old Cola Drinkers of America" formed to protest the new soda. The new pop flopped, a disaster for one of America's most successful companies.

RETURN OF THE CLASSIC

What the Coca-Cola Company didn't bank on was the power of passion and nostalgia. Many soda fans simply didn't want to bid farewell to a pop with a century of history,

or embrace a strange new taste. Less than 80 days after the announcement of the new formula, Coca-Cola execs admitted their mistake. They brought the original soda back. Called "Coke Classic," its reintroduction made the front page of newspapers across the country. The return of the classic formula put the company's soda back in the lead in the Cola Wars—a position it has maintained ever since.

NEW COKE

CLASSIC COKE

Lesson Learned

CHANGE ISN'T ALWAYS GOOD. Coke fans were happy with the original formula and passionate about protecting it—to the point of stockpiling cases of original Coke. If you ever consider transforming into a "new you," think about all the people who might miss the old you. No need to make radical changes to your fashion, personality, or any other aspect of your life if doing so might alienate your friends and family.

TRIUMPHANT TAKEAWAY If you're going to make a change, make sure it's an improvement.

McOops!

Fast food is a guilty pleasure: fast, tasty, and far from healthy. But when chain restaurants experiment with their menus, they end up with treats that seem more like gut-busting tricks …

HULA BURGER
McDonald's

If you think a beefy burger topped with a slice of grilled pineapple is a tropical treat, then this burger served with pineapple instead of beef is more like a trick. It's a recipe McDonald's founder Ray Kroc cooked up for his restaurant chain in the 1960s as an alternative for Catholics who don't eat meat on Fridays. Kroc learned quickly that these customers preferred the Filet-O-Fish to some strange fruit burger.

WAFFLE TACO
Taco Bell

Sausage and egg snuggled in a taco-shaped waffle might not sound like an authentic breakfast from south of the U.S. border, but Taco Bell's Waffle Taco was really more of an experiment for the chain's new breakfast menu. Although Ronald McDonald raved about the strange menu addition (actually, it was a regular guy who happened to be named Ronald McDonald in a clever ad campaign), the breakfast oddity was replaced a year later by the less exotic Biscuit Taco.

McSPAGHETTI
McDonald's

The ultimate American fast-food restaurant veered into Italian territory in the late 1970s, when McDonald's added spaghetti (and later, pizza) to its menu of Big Macs and fries. As you might expect, the dishes didn't exactly make customers exclaim, "Mama Mia!" The items disappeared quickly from the menu, although you can still order McSpaghetti in the Philippines and pizza in a few McDonald's restaurants.

PICKLE-O'S
Sonic

Deep-fried dill pickle slices are an actual thing in some parts of the United States. In fact, they're even a delicacy. Don't scrunch up your face! Drive-in restaurant Sonic put this oddball side dish on its menu in the 1960s, but Pickle-O's failed to catch on. If you get a craving, you can still order them off a secret menu in some Sonic restaurants in the southern United States.

HOT-DOG-STUFFED-CRUST PIZZA
Pizza Hut

Like an international food fair spilled across one hot pie, this eye-popping pizza has burgers and hot dogs cooked right into its crust, complete with mustard and ketchup drizzled on top. What's next? A pizza crust stuffed with a second pizza? It's been done! Called the "Double Sensation," the pizza within a pizza is available only in Singapore. Now that's a deep dish.

Instant Treats That Overheat?

Microwave burritos, instant mac and cheese, frozen pizza—fast-to-fix foods are lifesavers when you have a big appetite but little time. But at least two of these instant meals came with an extra serving of danger ...

ACHIN' BACON

If Reddi-wip whipped cream in a can is the most clever way to package food since, well, sliced bread (don't act like you haven't sprayed a glob of Reddi-wip right into your mouth), then Reddi-Bacon (from the same company) is one of the weirdest—and most dangerous. Introduced in 1964 as "real bacon that cooks in your toaster," Reddi-Bacon came precooked in tinfoil packages lined with spongy paper. The bacon cooked in minutes, but streams of grease dripped from the paper and clogged up toasters, creating a fire hazard. Oh no!

FRYER'S REMORSE

The opposite of fast food, Thanksgiving dinner is a belt-busting feast built around a centerpiece dish—roasted turkey—that takes at least three hours to cook. Naturally, savvy chefs have figured out a shortcut for serving up this 400-year-old tradition. The recipe is simple: dunk a medium-size turkey in a stockpot of cooking oil, then boil the bird for just a fourth of the time required to roast a turkey of similar size. Voilà! Deep-fried turkey is ready to serve.

When cooked correctly, this extra-crispy dish is finger-licking good. When cooked incorrectly, it's finger-burning bad. Roiling oil erupts from overfilled pots and singes skin. Half-thawed turkeys burst into flames when melting ice combines with the hot grease. Since 2002, turkey-frying mishaps have caused nearly 700 injuries. Which is why fire departments prefer that people cook their turkeys like the Plymouth colonists: slowly and safely.

Lesson Learned

TAKING THE FAST AND EASY WAY is fine most of the time, but sometimes you should slow down and smell the roses (or the bacon, or the coffee). Social media, microwave popcorn, pizza delivery in 30 minutes—modern life is full of opportunities for instant gratification. But you'll want to set these conveniences aside once in a while for two reasons: One, they won't always be available. Smartphone batteries die. The Internet goes out. Delivery drivers get lost.

But more importantly, two: Sometimes it's fun just to take things slow. Talk to friends face-to-face instead of texting. Bake something from scratch. Studies show that delaying gratification—skipping the small reward now for greater rewards later—is actually good for you.

 TRIUMPHANT TAKEAWAY Sometimes shortcuts short-circuit.

Bottled Water for Pets?

NICE TRY!

Pet owners pamper their pooches and kitties with everything from bacon-flavored jerky to robotic self-cleaning litter boxes. But even the most compulsive cat and dog people stopped short of buying these two extravagant (and failed) pet treats ...

Too Crazy for Cats

KITTY QUENCHER!

Designed to wet the whistle of Mr. Whiskers, Thirsty Cat! was a bubbly fish-flavored beverage enriched with vitamins for your feline companions. (A second beef-flavored water called Thirsty Dog! was made to hit the spot for Spot). The water came and went in 1994, proving that pet owners will avoid buying expensive water for an animal that's perfectly happy drinking from the toilet.

Too odd for Dogs

FORTUNE SNOOKIES!

Fortune Snookies dispensed pet-related wisdom in the form of hundreds of silly sayings ("Cats are not chew toys!" and "You had me at 'Here, boy!'") printed on each chicken-flavored treat. They even came in a container inspired by a Chinese takeout box, and no two boxes contained the same fortunes. The concept of fortune cookies for dogs might seem adorable until you contemplate the obvious: Dogs can't read. These cookies had no future.

Lesson Learned

KNOW YOUR AUDIENCE. Sure, Thirsty Cat! and Fortune Snookies were silly, but that's not why they flopped. The pet product marketplace is full of treats and toys that are goofy—but the super-successful ones all seem to fulfill a particular need for pet owners. They offer something that other products don't. Both Thirsty Cat! and Fortune Snookies failed that test.

Don't learn this lesson the hard way. Before you offer a service (tutoring, yard work, babysitting) or compete in anything (sports, multiplayer video games, belching contests), take time to confer with your potential clients and teammates. Offer something they need, and you'll write your own fortune snook—er, cookie.

 TRIUMPHANT TAKEAWAY Silly ideas can succeed, but they need to be useful.

LOSING COMBINATIONS

Failed Food Mash-Ups?

NICE TRY!

Tired of tortilla chips? Checked out on chicken fingers? Think your mac n' cheese is no longer the bees knees? Try these creative combinations, and your taste buds won't know what hit them!

SALAD

+

JELL-O

=

JELL-O FOR SALADS!

Cherry, strawberry banana, grape, tropical fruit, and even mixed fruit are perfectly edible flavors for Jell-O, the world's most wobbly snack. But in the 1960s, Jell-O's makers tried a terrible assortment of tastes, including seasoned tomato, celery, and mixed vegetable. Called Jell-O for Salads, it was an attempt to trick kids into eating their veggies. Silly Jell-O executives. Kids are too smart to fall for that one!

FUNKY FRIES!

Chocolate and peanut butter? Yum! Chocolate and potatoes? Umm ... These two foods were combined for Funky Fries, an "extreme" style of fried side dish aimed at kids in 2002. And the Frankenstein-style food experimentation didn't end there. Funky Fries also came in cinnamon flavor and the color blue, which you could dip in blue ketchup from the same company. Which begs the question: Aren't french fries delicious just the way they are? These odd spuds flopped and soon disappeared from store freezers.

CHOCOLATE

FRENCH FRIES

PEPSI A.M.!

Packed with nearly 30 percent more caffeine than the regular formula, Pepsi A.M. was released in 1989 as an alternative to coffee. But early risers preferred their morning jolt from a cup of joe rather than a sugary soda. And the "A.M." in the name made it seem like Pepsi A.M. was only suitable for slurping with the sunrise. The pop flopped and was taken off the market a year later, although today's popular "energy drinks" are the same idea with smarter marketing.

COLA

COFFEE

Happy Accidents

EPIC WIN!

Taste successes that started as messes ...

HOT EATS

The invention of microwave popcorn started with a gooey lump. Engineer Percy Spencer was tinkering with a magnetron for plane-detecting radar systems in 1945 when he felt a funny feeling in his pocket. Inside, he found that his chocolate bar had melted from exposure to microwaves—a special frequency of radio waves—emitted by the magnetron.

Intrigued by the melted chocolate, Spencer grabbed some popcorn kernels and held them in front of the magnetron. Suddenly, he was responsible for two world-changing inventions at once: a new type of fast-cooking oven and microwave popcorn. Spencer realized that microwaves can make liquids and fats vibrate, which creates heat that can cook foods faster than conventional ovens.

COLD TREATS

If you've ever accidentally left out food overnight, you probably ended up with a stinky mess (and possibly a pet ant colony). When Frank Epperson forgot to put away some food in 1905, he made snack history. And he was just 11 years old!

When Epperson was growing up in Oakland, California, U.S.A., he left a glass of powdered pop mix on his porch overnight with the mixing stick propped up in the glass. He remembered his drink the next morning, but he found that it had frozen solid after an unusually cold night. Hoping to salvage his soda, Epperson ran the cup under hot water. Pop! The primitive Popsicle slid from the glass, complete with the stirrer stick as a handle. It tasted terrific, even on a chilly morning. He called his new invention the Eppsicle—a name that never really stuck. When he patented his idea nearly 20 years later, he went with the catchier name of Popsicle. It originally came in just seven flavors. Today's Popsicles come in coconut, fudge, mango, and even pickle flavors.

Lesson Learned

 SOMETIMES COMPLETE ACCIDENTS lead to awesome (and delicious) discoveries. Microwave popcorn and Popsicles might not exist today if their inventors had simply chucked their sloppy snacks into the garbage. They realized they had stumbled onto something great, then worked to turn their messes into successes.

Likewise, inspiration might strike when you try to fix a flub. You might not invent the next great frozen treat, but maybe you'll figure out a better way to complete a chore or solve a problem plaguing you or your pals. Don't let that breakthrough idea get away! Analyze your error to see what you might salvage from it.

 TRIUMPHANT TAKEAWAY Some blunders can lead to wonders!

"Never give up. Failure and rejection are only the **first step** to succeeding."

—Basketball coach Jim Valvano

CHAPTER FIVE

Poor SPORTS

EVERYONE LOVES A WINNER. We give them trophies, pester them for autographs, carry them on our shoulders, and throw them parades. But winners wouldn't be winners without the losers. This chapter champions the cause of the nonchampion—competitors who choked in the heat of play, teams that seem cursed to failure, record attempts gone hilariously wrong, and leagues for sports too silly to succeed. Lovable losers, prepare for your parade ...

A Cursed Baseball Team?

UH-OH!

The Chicago Cubs baseball team once seemed unstoppable, the first team to win the World Series twice in a row (in 1907 and 1908). They haven't won a World Series since. Some believe the team is suffering from a curse that began when a goat walked into the ballpark. Fans have been trying to reverse the curse ever since ...

GETTING HIS GOAT

Tavern owner Billy Sianis made a buddy for life when a goat fell from a passing truck and wandered into his business in 1934. Sianis named the goat Murphy and made him the mascot of his establishment, which he renamed the Billy Goat Tavern. (It's a hot Chicago tourist spot today.) Sianis and his smelly goat were inseparable. But not everyone was glad about Murphy ...

MURPHY'S FLAW

In 1945, Sianis bought two tickets to see a Cubs World Series ballgame in Chicago's Wrigley Field. One of the tickets, of course, was for his best furry buddy, but field officials kicked out the goat after spectators complained he was stinking up the stands. Outraged, Sianis declared, "Them Cubs, they ain't gonna win no more." He stormed from the stadium, and his "Curse of the Billy Goat" has seemingly held sway ever since. The Cubs haven't won a World Series in more than 100 years.

REVERSING THE CURSE

Players who left the Cubs went on to win the World Series on other teams—teams that weren't so mean to goats. Meanwhile, Cubs fans and Wrigley Field officials have made many attempts over the decades to cure the curse, including ...

Creature Comforts: The Cubs have invited Billy Sianis's nephew and a pet goat to the field many times.

Goat Herding: Cubs fans have taken goats to the stadiums of rival teams and invoked a curse when the beast was barred from entering.

Goat Giving: A charity called "Reverse the Curse" donates goats to families in need across the world. (The families raise the goats for their milk and cheese.)

Success Rate: Zilch!

Lesson Learned

BELIEVE YOU WILL SUCCEED! The Cubs' run of rotten luck has more to do with the fans' mood in the stands than the rude rejection of a farm animal more than 70 years ago. Cubs players say they can sense the spectators' attitude—every gasp at a foul ball and boo for a bad play. That anxiety translates to pressure on the field, potentially leading to chokes—mistakes made because of frayed nerves. Maybe if the fans believed more in their team than in the Curse of the Billy Goat, the Cubs might win the series.

Doubt and negative feelings in your own life can lead to a "self-fulfilling prophecy." If you believe that you will fail at something, you're more likely to sabotage your own efforts and accept defeat. A positive attitude, on the other hand, has the opposite effect. Have faith in your abilities—and your ability to learn as you go—and you'll keep from cursing yourself.

TRIUMPHANT TAKEAWAY A positive attitude can lead to positive results.

Largest Smurf Party?

NICE TRY!

If breaking world records is your sport of choice then beware this cautionary tale: Nearly 400 men, women, children—even babies—who gathered in the seaside Croatian city of Split in 2008 found failure. They got together to break a bizarre record: the most people dressed as Smurfs, those itty-bitty cartoon characters from '80s cartoons and movies. But although this big blue group had the right look, they came up short in one crucial department: Smurfpower.

It Could Be Worse!

WHEN YOU'RE HAVING A LOUSY DAY,
just be glad you're not Tony Wright. This Englishman managed to stay awake for more than 11 days in 2007, breaking what he believed was a Guinness World Record. He woke up to the nightmarish dose of bad news: The official record was ten hours longer, and Guinness didn't even recognize sleep-deprivation records anymore!

OUT-SMURFED

Skim the Guinness World Records and you'll find all sorts of funky feats, including hurdling while wearing swim flippers, racing while hula-hooping, and the most people eating breakfast in bed simultaneously. Add to this ludicrous list "the most people dressed as Smurfs." The Croatian Smurfs thought they had the previous record—which they believed was 291—whupped. They even called TV and newspaper outlets to record the event.

It's too bad none of the Croatian Smurfs checked with the Guinness organization before donning their white caps. They didn't know it, but a new Smurf record was set the previous year by 451 students at England's University of Warwick. If only the Croatian group had invited another 57 wannabe Smurfs—an easy feat, according to the spokesperson for the group—they would have dressed in silly costumes for a reason. Instead of beating the record, the blue-faced Smurfs just ended up red in the face.

Attempts Gone Awry

Up and Away: French daredevil Michel Fournier was all set for his record-breaking high-altitude skydiving attempt when the balloon built to lift his jump module 21 miles (34 km) high detached and floated away without him.

Sticky Mess: Look out! It's a tidal wave of Popsicle slush! Beverage company Snapple sent New York City pedestrians scrambling in June 2005 when it attempted to beat the Guinness World Record for the world's largest Popsicle. The 25-foot (7.6-m)-tall kiwi-strawberry treat melted quickly in the heat, flooding the streets and sidewalks with sticky syrup. Firefighters were forced to close several streets and use their hoses to clean up the mess. The lesson here: Don't attempt the record for the world's largest Popsicle on the first day of summer.

Eatin' Defeat: More than a thousand cooks in 2008 were putting the finishing touches on the world's largest sandwich—4,921 feet long (1,500 m)—when the crowd of hungry spectators rushed in to devour the humongous hoagie before it could officially be measured.

Domino Effect: A Dutch team was *this* close to finishing their record-breaking attempt to topple four million dominoes when a panicked sparrow flapped into their work space and knocked over more than 20,000 of them.

Lesson Learned

MAKE SURE YOU KNOW—and learn from—what has been done before. The Croatian Smurfs' big mess-up was relying on outdated info from the Internet. A little more digging would have set the record straight, helping the blue group achieve Smurfing fame instead of Smurfing shame.

Although it's always easier to believe what you hear through the gossip grapevine or read online, take some time to verify the information and consider its source—especially if the information could hurt someone in your family or social circle. Rumors can do damage to somebody's reputation—or put you in an embarrassing situation—when they're wrong. If you're not sure something you heard or read is true, seek more sources.

TRIUMPHANT TAKEAWAY Do your research!

Sorry Sports Mash-Ups?

UH-OH!

Fed up with football? Basketball too boring? Need more excitement in your skydiving? Simple: Just add trampolines and wrestling moves (and toss in an ironing board while you're at it). What could go wrong? See for yourself …

BASKETBALL

TRAMPOLINE

SLAM BALL!

The ball wasn't the only thing bouncing off the court in this high-flying version of basketball. Trampolines set into the floor inside the free-throw line launched players into the air and turned every shot into a slam dunk contest—and an opportunity for sprains and bruises. Aerial spins and other stunts made for stunning slow-mo replays in televised games, but injuries and lack of fan interest eventually grounded SlamBall.

THE XFL!

As if professional football didn't have enough tough tackles, the "Xtreme Football League" offered fewer rules and more bone-rattling impacts. Games started with a mad scramble for the ball rather than a coin toss, but what would you expect from a sport created by the owner of the World Wrestling Federation? Lack of talent and an excess of injuries quickly sunk the league, which lasted for one season.

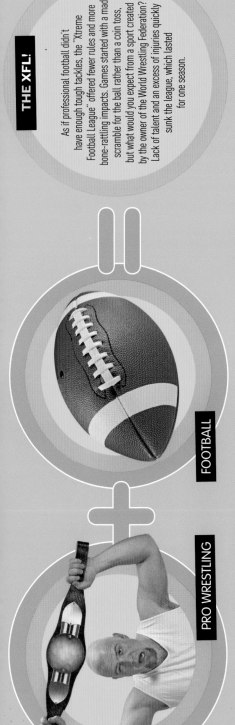

PRO WRESTLING + FOOTBALL

EXTREME IRONING!

Begun as a silly celebration of the art of multitasking (and wrinkle-free laundry), XTREME Ironing has evolved into a semiserious international sport with many disciplines: bungee jumping while ironing, skydiving while ironing, mountain climbing while ironing, even scuba diving while ironing! Competitors share photos of their most extreme ironing achievements on the official XTREME Ironing website. So far this sport has had just one world championship event, back in 2002.

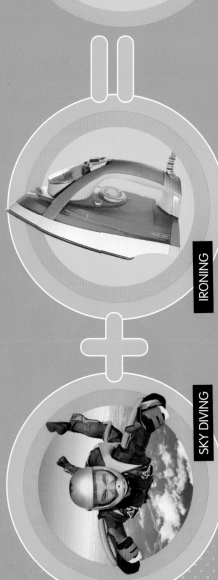

SKY DIVING + IRONING

Bobsledders From the Tropics?

OH NO!

World records were smashed and gold medals were grabbed at the 1988 Winter Olympics in Calgary, Canada, but the games' most memorable moments weren't created by the champions. Meet the lovable losers who were the real stars of the show ...

They were the ultimate underdogs: four men who grew up surrounded by sand and the sea, competing on a mountain of ice and snow against the world's greatest winter-sports athletes. They were Jamaica's first Olympic bobsledding team, assembled for the 1988 games to prove the prowess of the tropical island's competitors in any climate. Although Jamaica is famous for its track stars (speediest man alive Usain Bolt is from there), none of them wanted to compete in the dangerous sport of bobsledding. The team's founders turned to the military for brave competitors, including a sprinter to help push the sled and a helicopter pilot to steer it.

After finishing 30th out of 40 teams in the two-man event, the Jamaicans decided to compete in the four-man bobsled—despite lacking racing experience or even a four-person sled (they bought one from the Canadian team). A record crowd turned out to watch them compete. After an impressive start to the run, disaster struck. The bobsled bounced off the walls and flipped on its side, sliding to a halt. Spectators hushed as they waited to see if the Jamaicans survived the nasty crash. As each athlete emerged, shaken but unhurt, the crowd erupted into cheers. The Jamaicans shook hands with the crowd and accepted pats on the back as they pushed their bobsled to the finish line. They returned to their country as national heroes, inspiring a new generation of Jamaican bobsledders—including a women's team—that went on to find Olympic success. Their story was even made into a blockbuster movie: the 1993 Disney film *Cool Runnings*.

Lesson Learned

THE JAMAICAN BOBSLED TEAM won over the crowds with their determination and heart, if not their skills. You'd be surprised at how far your own derring-do and positive attitude will take you. You might not break any records or bring home a trophy, but you'll certainly impress your friends and family. Just as everybody loves a winner, they also love a loser who gives it their all. The success of the movie about the Jamaican bobsledders is proof enough of that.

TRIUMPHANT TAKEAWAY It's better to try and fail than to never have tried at all.

STRIKING OUT

OOPS!

After leading the Chicago Bulls to a "three-peat"—or the winning of three consecutive championships—Jordan shocked the sports world in 1993 by stepping off the basketball court and onto the baseball field. Jordan had grown tired of basketball. He was also devastated by the recent death of his father, who had dreamed that Jordan would become a major league baseball player. He signed a contract with the Chicago White Sox to play on its minor league farm teams. But although Jordan soared on the basketball court, he crashed on the baseball field. His batting, running, and fielding skills were not up to snuff for even minor league ball. Fans and teammates treated him with a mix of respect and curiosity, but the press was less kind. *Sports Illustrated* magazine called him an embarrassment to baseball.

Although Michael Jordan's abysmal season in minor league baseball was seen as a failure, the experience renewed his passion for basketball. In 1995, he returned to the Chicago Bulls and helped the team achieve another three-peat before retiring in 1999. He became a joker of the baseball diamond, but Jordan returned to the basketball court as its king.

Lesson Learned

YOU CAN LEARN A LOT when you leave your comfort zone. Trying something new, strange, or uncomfortable can teach you about your limits and focus your skills. Running for office at school, trying a dance class, giving a new sport a shot—any of these endeavors will teach new skills and test old ones. Maybe you'll fail and suffer a little embarrassment, or maybe you'll excel and learn that you actually like public speaking or T-ball or moving to the groove.

A Basketball Champ at Bat?

UH-OH!

He led his team to win six championships and took home eight awards for most valuable player (not to mention two Olympic gold medals), but Michael Jordan—aka MJ—is considered the world's greatest basketball player for more than just his stats. Jordan turned every shot into such an aerobatic performance that fans paid hundreds of dollars to wear a pair of his Air Jordan shoes. But after MJ learned to soar, he stumbled ...

Down but Not Out!

[BETHANY HAMILTON]

Even a shark attack couldn't stop surf champ Bethany Hamilton ...

In the competitive world of Hawaiian surfing, Bethany Hamilton was a rising star— a girl who could conquer the islands' treacherous curls. Although she was just 13 years old, Hamilton had already won two surfing championships. On a fall morning in 2003, she was catching waves at a popular surf spot with her best friend, Alana Blanchard. Hamilton relaxed on her board between sets, letting her arms dangle over the sides. Sea turtles swam nearby, and so did something much larger. The girls were not alone.

DEEP TROUBLE

The tiger shark that attacked Hamilton was as long as a minivan and one of the deadliest, most aggressive fish in the ocean. Its jaws had evolved to chomp through the shells of turtles, the tiger shark's favorite food. The attack was so fast that she didn't feel any pain or even realize she'd been bitten until the water around her began turning red. Barely able to paddle, Hamilton reached Blanchard's board and told her she'd been attacked. Blanchard

thought her friend was playing a mean joke—until she noticed Hamilton's left arm was gone.

SECOND WAVE

Fortunately, Blanchard's father and brother were surfing nearby. The Blanchards helped Hamilton ashore, then lashed a surfboard leash around her injured arm to stop the bleeding. By the time she reached the hospital, Hamilton had lost 60 percent of her blood.

Amazingly, though, she recovered from the attack. Not only was Hamilton determined to get back into the water as quickly as possible—she vowed to return to competitive surfing, despite her lost arm. Just three weeks after the shark bite, Hamilton was surfing again. At first she rode a custom board that was easier to paddle with one arm. Before long, she was back to riding a standard high-performance surfboard. Hamilton took fifth place in an Australian surfing competition in 2004. The following year, she won two consecutive surfing competitions. The fearless girl who conquered Hawaii's curls went on to conquer the surfing world.

Lesson Learned

MOST PEOPLE WHO LIVED through Hamilton's ordeal wouldn't dare dip a toe in the ocean, let alone dive back into a sport that requires upper-body strength and a cool head in wild waves. If Hamilton could get back in the water three weeks after a shark attack, then what's stopping you from doing ... well, anything? Need to give a speech in front of the whole class? No problem. Just got a tricky word in the spelling bee? You got this! Any time you need a little inspiration, just remember Bethany Hamilton—the girl who bounced back from a shark attack!

TRIUMPHANT TAKEAWAY Don't let fear keep you from going after your dreams!

"I was always in the **right place at the right time,** always willing to take advantage of an opportunity."

—Former con artist Frank Abagnale

CHAPTER SIX

Malfunctioning MISCHIEF

"There's a sucker born every minute," circus showman P. T. Barnum supposedly said. And although the saying might be true, you'd be making an honest mistake if you believed Barnum actually said it. (One of his competitors did.) This chapter is dedicated to the dishonest mistakes: crummy con artists, failed escape attempts, phony cure-alls, and other misdeeds aimed at "suckers" but ultimately undone.

A Pooch Impersonating a Lion?

OOPS!

A Chinese zoo had some explaining to do when the furry beast behind the bars of its "African lion" exhibit barked instead of roared. The zoo had pulled a switcheroo! And this lyin' lion wasn't the only counterfeit exhibit that the zoo's keepers tried to pass off ...

COPY CAT

 Hoping visitors wouldn't notice, keepers at the city zoo in Louhe, China, swapped their lion with a Tibetan mastiff dog: a burly, hairy breed. Well, people noticed! One visitor was trying to teach her six-year-old son about the different sounds that animals make when the lion started barking. The outraged woman felt like she was being ripped off. Zoo officials admitted they had sent their lion away to a breeding center and substituted it with the dog—a pet of one of the keepers.

Counterfeit Creatures

The lion wasn't the only animal imposter at Louhe's zoo. Visitors were surprised to find these other animal substitutes ...

The wolf exhibit contained a dog!

The snake case was home to two rats!

The leopard's den had a white fox!

Lesson Learned

ADMITTING THE TRUTH can be hard, but you shouldn't let a lie linger just to save your skin. The Louhe zoo was barely making enough money in ticket sales to cover its costs when visitors became outraged over its phony exhibits. The switcheroos hurt the zoo's reputation, which was bad for business.

When you're caught in a lie or exaggerate your abilities, your credibility takes a beating. Friends and family members might be less likely to trust you in the future. Be honest about what you have to offer as well as your shortcomings. Coming clean shows that you're trustworthy. It's a cliché to say that honesty is the best policy, but it's also the truth.

 TRIUMPHANT TAKEAWAY Don't try to deceive others just to save face.

A Cure-All That Cures Nothing?

NICE TRY!

Toothaches, migraines, joint pain, bug bites, scuffed knees—whatever the ailment or injury, a dab of Clark Stanley's Snake Oil Liniment would cure it. Or so Stanley promised. The self-proclaimed "Rattlesnake King" of Texas, U.S.A., traveled the West at the turn of the 20th century to hawk his miracle cure in front of crowds for 50 cents a bottle (a pretty penny for the time). But Stanley's "medicine" was more of a money-making scheme than a miracle cure ...

OIL RUSH

Most modern medications go through intense testing to make sure they heal instead of harm you. That wasn't the case in the early 1900s, when more than 30,000 cure-all concoctions were made and sold in the United States. Stanley was one of a new breed of slick-talking salespeople who pushed these potions, peddling them at fairs and selling them to drugstores. Stanley wowed the crowds at his "medicine shows" by slaying deadly rattlesnakes and wringing them of their fluids, which possessed healing powers according to Chinese and Native American lore.

Modern studies of snake fats show that these oils do pack some health-boosting properties, but Stanley's concoction and other snake oils of his day didn't have any medicinal value for a big reason: They didn't contain any snake oil! When government officials analyzed Stanley's liniment, they discovered it was mostly mineral oil, with a dab of beef fat and some nasty turpentine to make it smell like medicine. Which, of course, it wasn't. Authorities put Stanley out of business and cracked down on the sale of other snake oils—a term that has come to cover all useless concoctions marketed as cure-alls.

Lesson Learned

TRY TO BE A CRITICAL CONSUMER. Snake oil might be an old term for bogus medicine, but the idea is still very much alive. Late-night TV commercials and Internet pop-up ads are packed with products that promise to make you smarter or slimmer or peppier or better looking. But if these supplements and self-improvement gadgets really worked, don't you think they'd be easier to find than by channel surfing in the dead of night? Do a little product research before you break open your piggy bank.

BAD MEDICINE ## Three More Quack Attacks

Skull drilling: Since ancient times, healers have treated everything from headaches to troublesome thoughts by boring holes in their patients' skulls—a procedure called trepanation.

Spray-on hair: You've heard of canned air, but what about canned hair? Infomercials advertise spray-on hair-thickening powders that only resemble hair in dim light and wash away in a light rain.

Toning masks: Twenty-six electrified contacts inside these masks supposedly tighten the face and reduce wrinkles—and make the wearer look like a robot from a terrible sci-fi movie in the process!

TRIUMPHANT TAKEAWAY If something sounds too good to be true, it probably is.

Spell (Un)checked

OOPS!

Can you find the flubs in these photos?

MADE IN "AMERCIA"

A phone app for 2012 U.S. presidential candidate Mitt Romney offered a variety of upbeat slogans, one of which featured a curiously spelled country.

VEXING X-ING

The workers who painted this pedestrian-crossing sign on a street in front of a New York City high school might want to attend a few classes themselves.

The typo on this road sign in Oxfordshire, England, is bad enough. Imagine what would've happened if this road had closed during a month that was actually hard to spell, like Febroorarey!

I MAXXED

The managing director of Chile's mint made a career change after he approved 50-peso coins with an unfortunate misspelling. The highly collectible coins remain in circulation today.

Lesson Learned

TAKE YOUR TIME. If the unfortunate folks behind the silly mistakes in these photos had taken a second to proofread their work, you wouldn't be reading about them in a book called *Famous Fails!* You should always devote a tad extra time to each project—whether it's a school paper or even a status update—before unleashing it on the world. You'll be amazed at the mistakes you catch when you spend a few hours away from your writing project, for instance, and then review it with "fresh eyes." Another proofreading trick: Read through your work backward.

The benefits of double-checking extend beyond writing, too. The phrase "measure twice, cut once" applies to more than just carpentry, after all!

 TRIUMPHANT TAKEAWAY Spending more time now saves time later.

A Horse That's a Math Whiz?

NICE TRY!

At the beginning of the 19th century, crowds gathered in Berlin to watch a nine-year-old named Hans solve simple math problems, tell the time, distinguish musical tones, and accomplish other feats. The spectators were so astonished that Hans was given the nickname "Clever Hans." These tasks might not seem particularly clever—until you realize that Hans wasn't a human being; he was a horse! Hans was a sensation across Germany until experts discovered his secret. Turns out this horse was playing with his audience.

HOOFIN' IT

Clever Hans received his "education" from owner Wilhelm von Osten, a retired teacher who claimed he taught his horse the same way he once taught his human students (although we doubt von Osten rewarded schoolchildren with carrots and sugar cubes for correct answers). Tapping out his responses with his right hoof, Hans demonstrated an astounding mastery of a variety of subjects, including ...

• *Math!* Speaking in German or writing on a blackboard, von Osten would ask Hans to add, subtract, multiply, and divide, and Hans would stomp out the correct answer—even fractions.

• *Telling time!* Hans seemed able to read a watch and stamp out the correct time, right down to the minute.

• *Knowing the day!* Not only could Hans stamp out a number between one and seven to indicate the current day of the week, he could even identify the day after tomorrow or several days in the future.

• *Recognition!* Hans could identify people he'd been introduced to earlier by stamping out letters of the alphabet to spell their names. He could even identify objects and colors by stamping out codes von Osten developed.

HORSING AROUND

A German panel of experts—including a veterinarian, cavalry officer, and circus manager—investigated Clever Hans's supposed smarts in 1904. After detecting no tricks in von Osten's crowd-dazzling Q&A sessions, the panel concluded that Clever Hans lived up to his name. But then a psychologist named Oskar Pfungst noticed that something didn't add up. When Clever Hans was fitted with blinders or asked a question that the trainer didn't know the answer to, the horse suddenly stopped being clever. He just pawed the ground randomly, only getting the correct

answer 6 percent of the time as opposed to the usual 89 percent.

Pfungst came to a startling realization: Clever Hans wasn't an equestrian Einstein after all. He had been using his keen animal senses to read the body language and expressions of the people watching him. Whenever Hans stomped out the answers to questions, he could detect the subtle cues from his trainer and the spectators as he neared the correct response. By watching for these reactions, Hans gave his audience the answer they were expecting. He was still a clever horse—clever at scoring carrots and sugar cubes.

Lesson Learned

CLEVER HANS wasn't intentionally trying to trick anyone. He just wanted some treats, and his trainer didn't charge people for the show. It was all in good fun.

But sometimes people have more sinister motives for giving you only the answers you want. They might be trying to set you up for a scam. Or maybe they want to trick you into revealing some personal information or gossip about a friend. If you suspect someone is trying to butter you up, it's best to clam up.

TRIUMPHANT TAKEAWAY Beware when people tell you only what you want to hear.

A Jailbreak in a Pooch Costume?

UH-OH!

The history of prison breaks is filled with enough funny failures—jailbreakers who got stuck in their own chiseled escape holes, escapees caught because they couldn't resist posting on social media—to fill an entire book! But if there's one tale of attempted escape that tops them all, it's the time a man dressed as Snoopy tried to break into prison ...

COMIC RELIEF

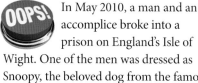

In May 2010, a man and an accomplice broke into a prison on England's Isle of Wight. One of the men was dressed as Snoopy, the beloved dog from the famous "Peanuts" comic strip. He was brandishing a squirt gun. Despite the intruder's silly costume, prison guards took the man seriously. After all, they thought the squirt gun was a real gun. The Snoopy imposter began banging on a door leading to staff offices. He hurled pieces of concrete at officers' cars.

It turns out he was trying to break a relative out of the prison. Clearly, his rescue plan had a few flaws (a giant cartoon dog isn't "exactly inconspicuous," said one prison official). Still, he might have succeeded in whisking away his imprisoned relative if not for one glaring problem: The Snoopy imposter had broken into the wrong prison. The two jailbreakers were arrested by the guards. The relative they had hoped to rescue remained behind bars at a nearby prison.

TRIUMPHANT TAKEAWAY If you can't do the time, don't do the crime.

A Phony Miracle Machine?

EPIC FAIL!

Imagine a machine that runs forever without any external source of power: no gas tank, no solar panels, no extension cord. Impossible, you say? Then you've already outsmarted Charles Redheffer, a con man who tried to trick everyone with this sham contraption—not once, but twice—more than 200 years ago.

DREAM MACHINE

In 1812, Redheffer arrived in Philadelphia, Pennsylvania, U.S.A., with a machine made of weights and spinning gears powering another smaller device that never seemed to stop. He claimed he had invented the fabled perpetual-motion machine, a self-powered mechanism that never stopped, and, if it were real, would have defied the laws of physics. Nevertheless, locals could pay to see it in action. When word spread of his revolutionary invention, Redheffer tried to cash in on his celebrity. He asked city officials for money to build a larger one.

The officials immediately became suspicious. Redheffer wouldn't let them inspect his machine from any closer than a barred window. But even from a distance, the inspectors noticed that the gears had a

ROBERT FULTON

Perpetual motion manufactory 1812. Robert Fulton

weird pattern of wear, suggesting that the smaller device was actually powering the larger perpetual-motion machine and not vice versa. To confirm their suspicions, the officials hired a local engineer to build a duplicate of Redheffer's machine with a hidden clockwork motor. They presented the machine to Redheffer, exposing him as a fraud.

But Redheffer wasn't ready to retire. He moved to New York City with a modified version of his machine and resumed his old tricks, charging people to see it. One of the spectators, an engineer named Robert Fulton, noticed something peculiar: The machine's movements were jerky, as if someone were powering it by hand.

When Fulton removed some loose boards from the wall next to the machine, he uncovered a belt. Following the belt's path through the wall, he discovered the machine's real power source: an elderly man in the attic turning a hand crank with one hand while snacking on bread with the other. A mob demolished Redheffer's machine after it was exposed as a fraud.

Lesson Learned

LISTEN TO THAT LITTLE VOICE in your head. It's trying to tell you something! Right from the start, Redheffer's skeptics sensed there was something off about his perpetual-motion machine. They listened to their instincts and exposed the scam.

Sometimes your own instincts might be trying to send you a message, too. Maybe something doesn't feel quite right about a person or situation. Or maybe your little voice is trying to push you into making a decision. It could be as simple as the answer in a multiple-choice test, or it might set you on the first step to achieving a long-term goal. Studies have shown that our gut reactions are often correct. You just need to listen.

TRIUMPHANT TAKEAWAY Trust your gut. It's usually right.

"It is **impossible to live** without failing at something, unless you live so cautiously that you might as well not have lived at all—in which case, you fail by default."

—*Harry Potter* author J. K. Rowling

CHAPTER SEVEN

POP CULTURE
Catastrophes

Imagine if your biggest mess-ups were on display for the masses. Your failures might be replayed for weeks on movie screens. Reporters would write about your missteps. The first thing that pops up when you search your name on the Internet would be your most embarrassing failure. Awkward! These are mistakes that have everyone talking: movie flops, fashion disasters, musical monstrosities, and attempts at fame that had everyone yelling two words: epic fail!

A Spider-Man Musical?

EPIC FAIL!

Web-slinging? Sure. Web-singing? Probably not Spider-Man's thing. The crime-fighting wall-crawler learned this lesson the hard way when he starred in *Spider-Man: Turn Off the Dark,* a musical take on Peter Parker's transformation from science nerd to superhero. It was both a wonderful spectacle and a blunder-filled spectacular. Browse the tangled web of one of the most troubled productions in Broadway history ...

WEBBED WONDER

Combining the explosive action of a Hollywood blockbuster with the live performance of a Broadway musical, *Spider-Man: Turn Off the Dark* featured battles above the audience (the show had nearly 40 aerial stunts, some of which even spilled into the aisles) and a high-tech New York City set that transformed right before the audience's eyes. With music composed by members of the rock band U2 and the same director as the Broadway hit *The Lion King,* it should have been the greatest show on Earth.

ACCIDENTS HAPPEN

Even before the show opened in 2011, its producers and actors learned that with great production values come great responsibility. Two stuntmen took painful tumbles while rehearsing the show's swinging sequences. In previews, the show often ground to a halt for technical malfunctions: cables falling on the audience, set pieces gone amiss, and at least one glitch that left an actress dangling above the audience for eight minutes. The list of actor injuries—concussions, broken wrists, crushed feet, busted ribs—seemed more in line with professional wrestling than a Broadway show. At least five actors were injured over the course of the production, which became the butt of jokes on and off Broadway for its risky sequences.

SHOWSTOPPER

Although audiences generally liked *Turn Off the Dark,* critics griped about its confusing plot and constant technical glitches. Meanwhile, behind the scenes, the show's creators and actors squabbled in lawsuits. The script was tweaked and action scenes were simplified for safety reasons, but by that point *Turn Off the Dark* couldn't turn on the charm. The most expensive musical in history didn't take in enough money at the box office to pay for itself. It closed in early January 2014 after suffering record-breaking losses.

It Could Be Worse!

CHRISTOPHER TIERNEY

WHEN YOU'RE HAVING A LOUSY DAY, just be glad you weren't Christopher Tierney. This *Spider-Man* stuntman tumbled more than 20 feet (6.1 m) into the orchestra pit during a live show of *Turn Off the Dark* (crew members forgot to attach his safety harness properly). Fortunately, Tierney was as tough as the character he played. Despite broken ribs and internal bleeding, he made a full recovery.

Lesson Learned

SIMPLE IS BEST. *Turn Off the Dark* became a Broadway legend—and an expensive lesson—for its out-of-control costs and overly complicated plot, stunts, and set design. A Spider-Man comic set to music should have been a surefire hit (*Shrek* and *The Lion King* were crowd-pleasing Broadway blockbusters), but *Turn Off the Dark's* creators shoehorned in too much spectacle. The result: an expensive mess.

Whenever you start a creative endeavor (such as writing a story, building a tree house, or designing a science-fair project), resist the urge to fill it with frills and unnecessary details (at least at first). The more complicated you make something, the more things can go wrong. You can get lost among all the moving parts and lose track of the big picture: to create something cool.

TRIUMPHANT TAKEAWAY Sometimes less is more. Keep things simple.

Crimes of Fashion

UH-OH!

Some fashions last. These did not. Here's a head-to-toe history of fashion's biggest failures...

MACARONI WIGS

Ancestors of the modern hipster, macaronis (named for their love of the Italian noodle) were young 19th-century Englishmen famous for their silly sense of humor and a fashion sense that was literally over the top. They wore towering wigs covered in white powder and crowned with teeny-tiny hats that could only be removed with a long stick or the point of a sword.

WOMEN'S SHOULDER PADS

A style intended to project power in the business world, shoulder pads were sewn into women's suits and blouses throughout the 1980s. They combined the cutthroat attitude of a Wall Street banker with the fashion sense of an Oakland Raiders linebacker. Fortunately, the fad faded (although smaller shoulder pads still surface in women's fashion today).

FANNY PACKS

Also known as bum bags, waist bags, and butt packs (depending on where in the world you wear them), fanny packs are big enough to carry cameras, tissues, wallets, makeup,

96

and other essentials in a hands-free bag worn around the waist, either below the belly or above the butt. Practical? Yes. Fashionable? Never. Today they're the trademark accessory of tourists or really anyone who doesn't care how they look.

CARPENTER PANTS

Designed with loops and deep pockets for holding hammers and other tools, carpenter jeans are practical pants for woodworkers and construction crews. But fashion police called foul in the early 2000s when carpenter pants became popular among teens and twentysomethings who appreciated their baggy fit for dancing.

BAREFOOT RUNNING SHOES

These rubber shoes were designed to fit your feet like a glove and enhance running abilities. Some long-distance runners swear by them, despite the shoes needing a lengthy break-in time. Barefoot shoes made this list for two reasons: They've been shown to offer no benefit over regular running shoes, and they're downright freaky!

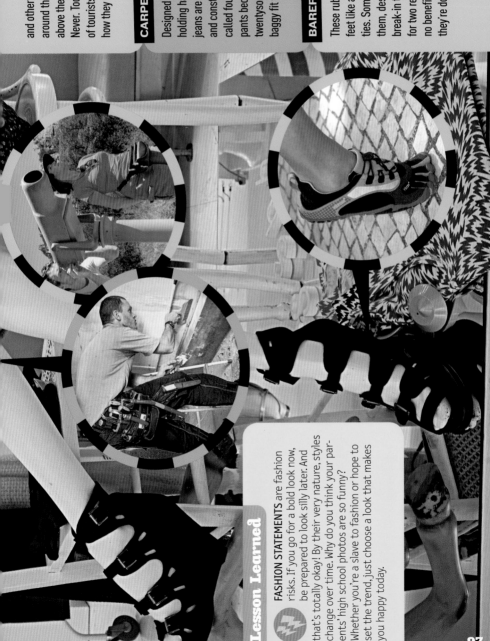

Lesson Learned

FASHION STATEMENTS are fashion risks. If you go for a bold look now, be prepared to look silly later. And that's totally okay! By their very nature, styles change over time. Why do you think your parents' high school photos are so funny? Whether you're a slave to fashion or hope to set the trend, just choose a look that makes you happy today.

97

Flick Fails

OOPS!

OOPS!

Can you the spot the screwups in these movies?

Pssst! Your favorite films contain some dirty little secrets: flubs that slipped past the director's nose and made it to the screen. Scan these scenes and you'll never unsee them again ...

COWBOY ON DECK

AS SEEN IN: *Pirates of the Caribbean: The Curse of the Black Pearl*
LOCATION IN THE FILM: In the final scene

Captain Jack Sparrow's motley crew of scallywags was joined by a member of the film's actual crew—a man wearing a white cowboy hat.

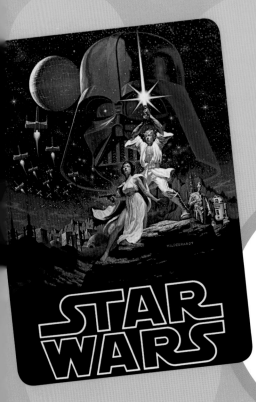

STORMTROOPER BLOOPER

AS SEEN IN: *Star Wars Episode IV: A New Hope*
LOCATION IN THE FILM: Around 1 hour, 22 minutes

While the film's heroes struggle to escape the Death Star's trash compactor, watch for a trio of stormtroopers to enter the compactor's control room. That trooper on the right clearly forgot to duck!

TENTACLE TALE

AS SEEN IN: *The Goonies*
LOCATION IN THE FILM: Near the end

When the adventurous kids of the Goonies gang are reunited with their parents at the end of the movie, one of the kids talks about his scary run-in with "the octopus." There's just one problem: The Goonies never encounter an octopus in the movie (the scene was cut from the film).

CAMERA MANNED

AS SEEN IN: *Harry Potter and the Chamber of Secrets*
LOCATION IN THE FILM: During the wizards' duel between Harry and Draco Malfoy

Blink and you'll miss this accidental shot of a cameraman kneeling with Hogwarts' students watching Harry and Draco duke it out. Guess he forgot to wear his invisibility cloak.

Lesson Learned

THE BLOOPERS in these movie scenes slipped past an army of effects artists, editors, and eagle-eyed directors. They're not immune to slipups, and neither are you. You're bound to make typos in your writing, for instance, or let a goal get past you in the soccer game once in a while.

Such mistakes might seem like the worst thing ever when they happen, but no one else is obsessing over them. Need proof? Everyone remembers the movies on these pages for their great stories and amazing characters, not a few silly mistakes. You're the only person who will focus on your own little screwups. So do yourself a favor: DON'T!

 TRIUMPHANT TAKEAWAY Don't beat yourself up over little mistakes.

A 30-Second
Fourth
of July?

EPIC FAIL!

Blink and you might've missed
one of the most explosive fireworks
displays of all time—if you weren't
too busy ducking for cover!

Talk about a short fuse. Imagine a half-hour Independence Day display—tens of thousands of high-flying fireworks, earth-shaking shells, and an explosive grand finale—all squeezed into just 30 seconds. Does that sound terrifying or terrific? Maybe both? Half a million people on the shores of San Diego Bay, California, U.S.A., witnessed this awesome spectacle on July 4, 2012, at an annual event called the Big Bay Boom. More than any previous year, this show lived up to its name. And it wasn't intentional.

The fireworks company responsible for the short-fused show traced the problem to a virus in the computer controlling the timing of the fireworks. Instead of going off gradually and building to a crescendo according to a carefully choreographed routine, all the fireworks ignited at once—five minutes before the show was supposed to begin—on barges scattered around San Diego Bay. The concentrated firepower sent a deep rumble through downtown San Diego. Fortunately, nobody got hurt, and everybody saw a display they would never forget!

Lesson Learned

OWN UP TO YOUR ERRORS. The company behind the fireworks mishap apologized to the spectators and took full responsibility. They even offered to put on the following year's show for free. How would you have felt if the company's officials had simply laid the blame on faulty software? They would likely have gone out of business with a bang—and a whimper.

Admitting you messed up isn't always easy, but it's a far better option than simply shrugging your shoulders and passing the blame. You might get a little grief for your mistake, but at the same time you'll earn respect for your honesty. Long after everyone forgets about your stumble, they'll remember you as a stand-up person.

TRIUMPHANT TAKEAWAY Don't pass the buck. Claim your mistakes.

Down but Not Out!

[J. K. ROWLING]

How the wizard behind Harry Potter overcame her cursed past ...

Today, Joanne "J. K." Rowling is one of England's wealthiest people and its most famous modern author. Her seven Potter novels have spawned blockbuster movies and even a theme park. But before Rowling's boy wizard cast his spell on the world, she had to overcome rejection and lean times that she termed "rock bottom." Here's how the world's most famous muggle conjured success from failure ...

WRITER BLOCKED

It's hard to believe anyone wouldn't be wild about Harry Potter today, but in the mid-1990s, Rowling had a tough time finding takers for her enchanting tale of witchcraft and wizardry, which she wrote on an old typewriter. Low on money and raising her daughter alone, Rowling saw her story rejected 12 times. Finally, an editor at a publishing company showed the first chapter of her manuscript to his eight-year-old daughter, who couldn't wait to read what happened next. *Harry Potter and the Philosopher's Stone* (known as *Harry Potter and the Sorcerer's Stone* in the United States) was published in 1997. The book became a smash with legions of readers who—just like the editor's daughter—couldn't wait to see what happened next.

WRITE RIGHT

Rowling's Writing Advice

READ, THEN WRITE: Rowling recommends reading as much as you can, as often as you can.

WRITE OFTEN: Try to write every day, even if it's just for ten minutes.

IT'S OKAY TO STINK: Rowling admits that she "wasted a lot of trees" before writing anything she really liked.

J. K. ROWLING

Lesson Learned

IF AUTHOR ROWLING had given up after getting her first rejection letter, the world wouldn't have its most beloved boy wizard today. And Rowling's persistence started well before her first batch of rejections. She knew she was on to something the moment Harry Potter sparked to life in her imagination as she was riding a train from Manchester to London in 1990. She began writing the book during a trying time: Rowling's own mother was dying of an illness, which inspired her tale of an orphan's battle with evil.

Rowling kept going: improving her writing, shaping her story, and then facing down the rejection. She saw failure as part of the creative process. That applies to you, too. If you believe in your abilities and work on improving your skills, you'll see each mistake for what it is: a stepping-stone to success. Not everyone is going to get where you're going, but if you believe in yourself (and ask for feedback from friends you trust), you'll eventually find success.

TRIUMPHANT TAKEAWAY If at first you don't succeed ... well, you know what to do.

"You **can't be that kid** standing at the top of the waterslide, overthinking it. You have to go down that chute."

—Comedian and actress Tina Fey

CHAPTER EIGHT

Lessons in LOSING

Give yourself a pat on the back—and not just because you're nearly finished with *Famous Fails!* You've messed up a few times in your life. By now you've learned that making mistakes can make you better, stronger, and smarter. So, congrats on all the missteps! This final self-help chapter will help you cope with your screwups, so you can pick yourself up and keep going.

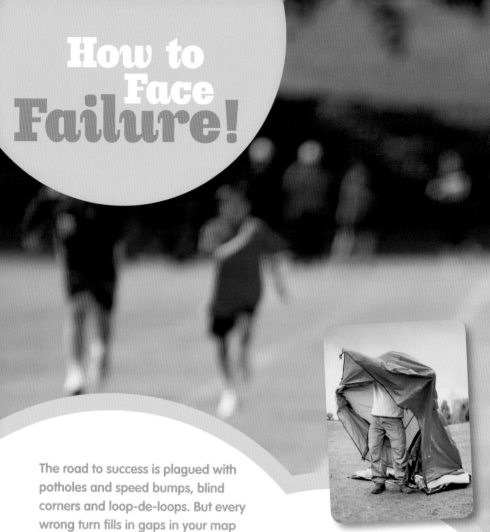

How to Face Failure!

The road to success is plagued with potholes and speed bumps, blind corners and loop-de-loops. But every wrong turn fills in gaps in your map and gets you one step closer to your destination. Heed these tips to fail better and keep moving forward …

FAILURE STINGS, AND THAT'S OKAY!

1 Some people treat failure like a dirty word, one never spoken out loud lest it crash your self-confidence. But research shows that feeling great about yourself doesn't necessarily lead to good grades or career growth or other measures of success. On the other hand, achieving success can actually boost your self-esteem. So, instead of ignoring failure just because it's painful, you should accept it, learn from it, and move on. Eventually you'll find success, a more natural way to boost your confidence.

FAILURE IS THE BEST TEACHER!

2 Failure has so many fans, it even has a convention: FailCon! Held in dozens of cities around the world, it's a daylong gathering of entrepreneurs, designers, investors, and other professionals who share lessons learned from their failures. They've embraced the teaching power of screwing up. Every mistake makes you smarter, not only by teaching you something you didn't know, but also something you *didn't know* you didn't know.

THE BEST MEASURE OF SUCCESS IS **HOW YOU DEAL WITH FAILURE!**

3 Think back to when you learned to ride your bike. Did you give up the first time you toppled over? Every mistake was like a roadblock—an excuse to give up. How you deal with such slipups will determine your chances of success. When you fell over on your bike, you weren't a failure unless you decided to stay down and give up. But you hopped back on and kept trying. It took courage, but eventually you stopped falling.

Failure IS an Option!

It teaches valuable lessons.

It keeps pushing you forward.

It shows you where you are in the process.

It's rarely a big deal.

It makes you appreciate your success all the more.

107

RESISTING SMALL REWARDS NOW LEADS TO BIG REWARDS LATER!

4 In a famous experiment that began in 1968 (and continues today), children were given the choice of eating one marshmallow whenever they wanted or waiting for the psychologist to return with two marshmallows. Participants with the patience to wait were shown to have better self-control and were able to better handle the frustration that comes with failure. They went on to attend better colleges and have more rewarding careers. The lesson here is that good things come to those who wait. The fast, easy solution isn't always best. A little patience goes a long way in solving problems and achieving long-term success.

ASK FOR HELP, NOT FOR PRAISE!

5 Praise might boost your confidence, but that's not going to help you solve a persistent problem. (And failing at that problem will eat away at your confidence, putting you right back where you started.) Your friends and family are there to help you! They can see the problem from a fresh perspective and give you honest advice. It takes courage to ask for help, but then it also takes brains to learn from your mistakes. Just remember to return the favor: When your friends or siblings ask for help, hook them up!

Zeroes to Heroes!

JENNIFER HUDSON

This terrific trio failed hard before they hit it big. Discover the inspiring secrets behind their astounding career turnarounds …

IDOL REVIVAL
Jennifer Hudson

As a successful singer, songwriter, and actress, Jennifer Hudson has conquered the showbiz world and taken home every major award, from an Oscar for acting to a Grammy for her music. Not bad for a former cruise-ship performer who didn't make the cut on a TV talent show. Although this singer from Chicago wowed the crowd with her powerful voice on *American Idol* in 2004, she only made it to seventh place before the TV audience voted her off.

If anything, Hudson's early exit from *American Idol* actually helped her career. Her fans were outraged when she was kicked off the show, and she has since been chosen as one of *American Idol*'s greatest contestants. Never doubting her abilities, Hudson continued to sing professionally after *American Idol* and pursued a record deal. Her big break came when she beat out hundreds of other actresses to play Effie White in the musical *Dreamgirls*, for which she won an Academy Award. Hudson later overcame a family tragedy to continue her unstoppable success. Today she's one of the most admired women in show business.

HOW SHE BOUNCED BACK:
By believing in herself!

ANCHOR MANAGEMENT
Katie Couric

She made millions of fans as the co-host of a popular morning news show, then made history as the first woman to anchor a nightly newscast. But long before TV journalist Katie Couric earned raves on every major network, she received a scathing review for her first on-air appearance. A network executive insisted he never wanted to see Couric on TV again. Barely a year out of college, Couric's career was almost over before it started.

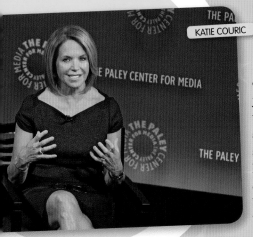

While his competitors from other countries made the dangerous sport of ski jumping look effortless, Eddie the Eagle wobbled through the air and pulled off shaky landings that put a lump in every spectator's throat. The crowds went wild for his unbeatable attitude and unbelievable daring, and Eddie joined the Jamaican bobsledders as a breakout star of the 1988 Winter Olympics. His reputation as a geeky good sport earned him fame and opportunities after the games—including recording a hit song and a movie about his life.

HOW HE BOUNCED BACK:
By embracing his weaknesses!

Couric focused on the quality of her reporting, putting together award-winning stories for a local TV station. Her work earned her respect and promotions, and in 1991 she was made co-host of NBC's *Today Show.* "Experiencing setbacks, disappointments and, yes, failure helps you develop another essential skill," Couric told students at the University of Wisconsin, "and that's resilience."

HOW SHE BOUNCED BACK:
Through hard work!

SOAR LOSER
Eddie the Eagle

With his thick glasses and goofy grin, Michael Edwards didn't look like your typical Olympic athlete. He didn't train like one, either. The former plaster worker from England learned to ski jump in borrowed equipment (he wore six pairs of socks to make his boots fit) while wearing a helmet held on with a string. His soaring abilities earned him the nickname "Eddie the Eagle" and a spot at the 1988 Winter Olympics as Great Britain's first Olympic ski jumper. But this Eagle didn't land any medals in Calgary. In fact, he came in dead last.

EDDIE THE EAGLE

Keeping Cool Under Pressure

It happens to the best athletes at the worst times. It can make whiz kids feel like their brains just turned to mush. You probably know the feeling: When the stakes are high or someone is scrutinizing your every move, simple tasks become supertricky. You miss the pop fly, mess up the math problem on the chalkboard, forget your lines in the school play, or mangle an easy word in a spelling bee. Uh-oh! You just choked under pressure.

OOPS! Choking is a real—and heavily studied—phenomenon. Experiments on athletes and students have helped to reveal the reasons why we choke, including a quirk in human memory that actually sabotages simple tasks. But the most common cause is simple: We think too much, distracting ourselves from what should be a simple task. The good news is we can unlock these mental blocks. In her book *Choke*, psychologist Sian Beilock has studied this enemy of success and suggested many fixes, including ...

DURING SPORTS

1. Distract Yourself From Distraction

Sports history is chock-full of chokes: pro golfers who missed the easy putt, gold medalists who stumbled at the finish line, baseball teams cursed by farm animals (remember the Chicago Cubs?). Beilock believes athletes who choke were thinking too much about what they were doing—a problem she calls "paralysis by analysis." Sinking a putt and catching a ball are automatic processes for the pros, but such simple tasks become complicated when athletes stop to ponder the process. The solution: distraction! Humming a tune, whistling, or focusing on some bland detail like the color of an opponent's uniform is often all it takes to put athletic skills back on automatic.

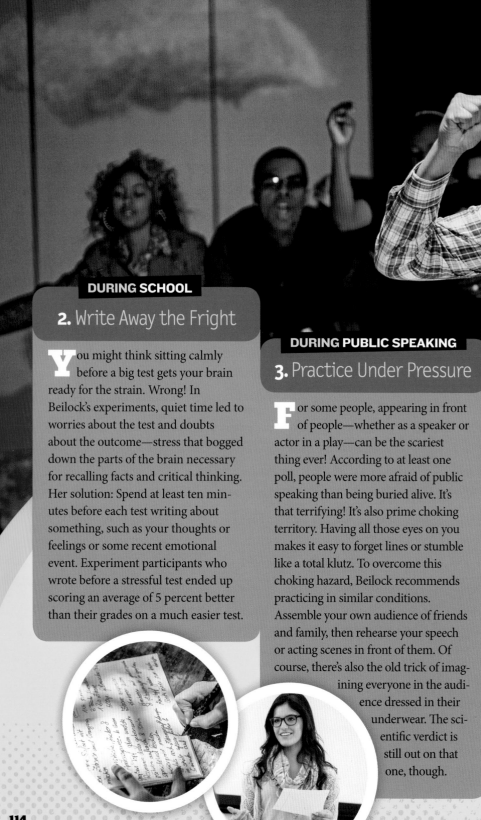

2. Write Away the Fright

You might think sitting calmly before a big test gets your brain ready for the strain. Wrong! In Beilock's experiments, quiet time led to worries about the test and doubts about the outcome—stress that bogged down the parts of the brain necessary for recalling facts and critical thinking. Her solution: Spend at least ten minutes before each test writing about something, such as your thoughts or feelings or some recent emotional event. Experiment participants who wrote before a stressful test ended up scoring an average of 5 percent better than their grades on a much easier test.

DURING PUBLIC SPEAKING

3. Practice Under Pressure

For some people, appearing in front of people—whether as a speaker or actor in a play—can be the scariest thing ever! According to at least one poll, people were more afraid of public speaking than being buried alive. It's that terrifying! It's also prime choking territory. Having all those eyes on you makes it easy to forget lines or stumble like a total klutz. To overcome this choking hazard, Beilock recommends practicing in similar conditions. Assemble your own audience of friends and family, then rehearse your speech or acting scenes in front of them. Of course, there's also the old trick of imagining everyone in the audience dressed in their underwear. The scientific verdict is still out on that one, though.

Silly Mash-Ups That Succeeded

YIPPEE!

You laughed at some madcap mergers (Chocolate french fries! Aerial ironing!) earlier in the book, but some combinations are so crazy that they actually worked! Behold these bizarre blends that bucked the losing trend ...

BEAN BAG

PANDA

BEANIE BABIES!

More than half the households in America owned at least one of these in the 1990s. It wasn't because they were particularly cute or pleasing to squeeze. It was creator Ty Warner's billion-dollar formula: releasing Beanie Babies in limited quantities, making them hard to find and extremely collectible. A black market blossomed on Internet auction sites, with rare Beanie Babies selling for thousands of dollars. Eventually, the fad ran its course and the Beanie Baby business collapsed—but Warner walked away as one of the world's richest men.

CHESS BOXING!

A battle of fists and wits, chess boxing involves alternating rounds of hand-to-hand combat and head-to-head strategy on the chess board. Victory is achieved by either knockout or checkmate. And not only is this ludicrous mash-up a real thing, it's actually growing in popularity, with its own international organization and world championships.

BOXING

CHESS

PET ROCK!

In 1975, a California, U.S.A. ad writer named Gary Dahl invented the "Pet Rock" after complaining about all the chores—walking, feeding, pooperscooping—involved with keeping a dog or cat. Dahl joked that it was the perfect pet for the lazy owner! His silly scheme became the must-give gift for the holidays, earning him millions. He packaged each rock (which he bought for about a penny) in a cardboard box complete with ventilation holes and an owner's manual packed with funny facts and training info. It sold for $3.95. The easiest trick to teach a Pet Rock? Playing dead.

DOG

ROCK

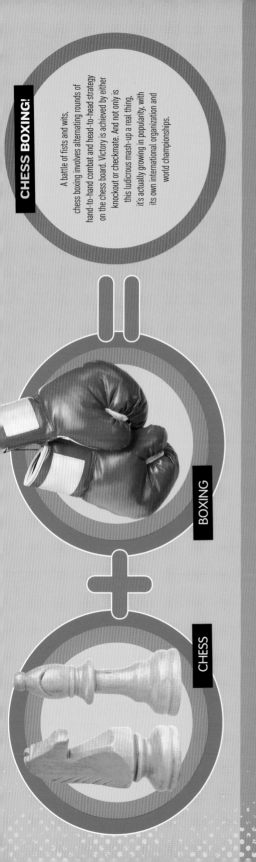

Built to Laugh

OOPS! If failure is crucial to success, then why not try succeeding at failure? There's even an art to it. Welcome to the weird world of chindōgu (pronounced chin-doh-goo), Japanese for "unusual tool." The brainchild of Japanese inventor Kenji Kawakami, chindōgu celebrates inventions that are both real and surreal, somewhere between useful and useless. In fact, chindōgu inventions are often described as unuseless because they solve a problem but often create other problems when you use them.

KENJI KAWAKAMI

Confused? The best way to understand the concept is to see it for yourself and try to make your own impractical gadget (a solar-powered flashlight, perhaps, or a package of dehydrated water). Chindōgu inventions are scattered across these pages for inspiration. Devising your own—whether just drawing it on paper or actually making it from items you already have—can be both fun and a lesson in how to fail and succeed. But before you dream up your unusual tool, make sure to follow these simple rules from Kawakami himself ...

Chindōgu Rules

It must be possible to actually make the device.

You can almost imagine someone actually using it.

You're not allowed to sell or patent your invention.

It mustn't be invented just for a joke and must solve a normal, real-world problem.

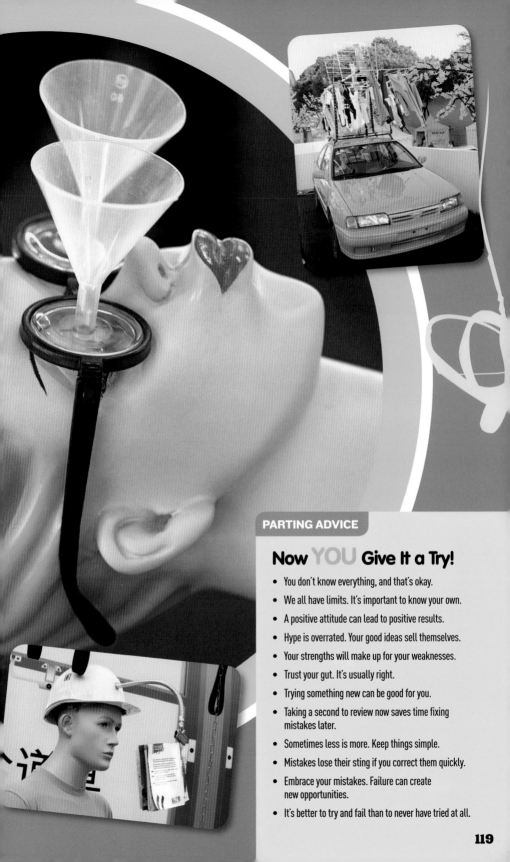

Now YOU Give It a Try!

- You don't know everything, and that's okay.
- We all have limits. It's important to know your own.
- A positive attitude can lead to positive results.
- Hype is overrated. Your good ideas sell themselves.
- Your strengths will make up for your weaknesses.
- Trust your gut. It's usually right.
- Trying something new can be good for you.
- Taking a second to review now saves time fixing mistakes later.
- Sometimes less is more. Keep things simple.
- Mistakes lose their sting if you correct them quickly.
- Embrace your mistakes. Failure can create new opportunities.
- It's better to try and fail than to never have tried at all.

Answer Key

Page 19: Oops! Did you catch that thumbs-down that was supposed to be a triumphant thumbs-up?

Page 29: Upside down alert! This image is supposed to be right side up.

Page 43: Do you no how to spell? Whoops! It's "know" not "no"! This one's another mis-spelling: "Leraned" should be "Learned"!

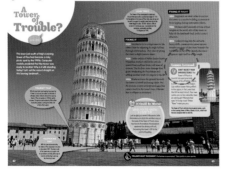

Page 47: 1, 2, 3, 4, 6. Wait! That's not right! If you caught this one then you deserve a high five!

Page 58: Something looks not-so-right about this number! It needs to be rotated to the right to make it right!

Pages 74-75: These pages might have thrown you a curveball. Well, you're right. They're upside down!

Page 81: This rat isn't climbing on the ceiling, it's just upside down!

Page 98: Two speech bubbles each saying the same thing? Double oops is right!

Page 116: Another speech bubble snafu—we printed the words in this bubble backward!

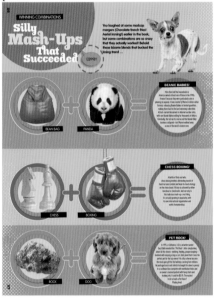

Index

Boldface indicates illustrations.

Index

Credits

DEDICATED TO ANYONE WHO HAS EVER TRIPPED ON A SIDEWALK, THEN BROKEN INTO A SORT OF SKIP-HOP DANCE THING AS IF THEY HAD TOTALLY MEANT TO DO THAT, FOOLING NO ONE. —C.B.

Since 1888, the National Geographic Society has funded more than 12,000 research, exploration, and preservation projects around the world. The Society receives funds from National Geographic Partners LLC, funded in part by your purchase. A portion of the proceeds from this book supports this vital work. To learn more, visit www.natgeo .com/info.

For more information, visit nationalgeographic .com, call 1-800-647-5463, or write to the following address:
    National Geographic Partners
    1145 17th Street N.W.
    Washington, D.C. 20036-4688 U.S.A.

Visit us online at nationalgeographic.com/books

For librarians and teachers: ngchildrensbooks.org

More for kids from National Geographic: kids.nationalgeographic.com

For information about special discounts for bulk purchases, please contact National Geographic Books Special Sales: ngspecsales@ngs.org

For rights or permissions inquiries, please contact National Geographic Books Subsidiary Rights: ngbookrights@ngs.org

Design/Art Direction by James Hiscott, Jr.

Paperback ISBN: 978-1-4263-2548-9
Reinforced library binding ISBN: 978-1-4263-2549-6

Printed in China
16/PPS/1

ILLUSTRATION CREDITS

EVERYBODY HAS THEIR UPS & DOWNS

Get the story on how these amazing guys and gals succeeded and inspired others to do the same!

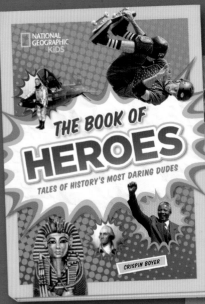

NATIONAL GEOGRAPHIC KIDS

THE BOOK OF HEROES

TALES OF HISTORY'S MOST DARING DUDES

CRISPIN BOYER

HEROES OF GEEK MYTHOLOGY

THE BENEVOLENT BILLIONAIRE:
Bill Gates

THE MAD SCIENTIST:
Nikola Tesla

THE FACE OF SPACE:
Neil deGrasse Tyson

GREAT GIFTS!

Amelia EARHART

FOR THIS GUTSY GAL, THE SKY WAS NO LIMIT

SKY-HIGH DREAMS

BREAKING BARRIERS

INTO THIN AIR

FEARLESS FACTS

STRANDED: DID AMELIA EARHART SPEND HER DAYS AS A CASTAWAY?

NATIONAL GEOGRAPHIC KIDS

THE BOOK OF Heroines

TALES OF HISTORY'S GUTSIEST GALS

STEPHANIE WARREN DRIMMER

NATIONAL GEOGRAPHIC KIDS